Chandler  Farquhar

**Dealers in Tools and Supplies**

March 1st, 1896 Supplement

Chandler  Farquhar

**Dealers in Tools and Supplies**
*March 1st, 1896 Supplement*

ISBN/EAN: 9783337202231

Printed in Europe, USA, Canada, Australia, Japan

Cover: Foto ©Andreas Hilbeck / pixelio.de

More available books at **www.hansebooks.com**

# ENDS *AND* ODDS.

OUR customers often see things in our stock not shown in any catalogue, and we trust, in making up your orders, you will not confine yourself to the articles only that we mention.

We aim to keep abreast of the times and add to our stock any article of merit, as soon as ready for the public.

A great many of these tools can be sent by mail, and we ask customers to enclose what you think would be right, including postage, and the balance, if any, will be returned to you.

We take pleasure in sending any of our catalogues to prospective customers, and shall esteem it a favor to have our goods brought to the notice of your acquaintances.

Everything, no matter how small, will receive attention.

## THESE PRICES ARE NET CASH.

We keep a large assortment of

CARPENTERS' HAMMERS, PLANES, BITTS, &c.,

MACHINISTS' HAMMERS, SQUARES, CALIPERS, &c.,

BLACKSMITHS' HAMMERS, TONGS, STEEL, &c.,

JEWELERS' PLYERS, FILES, MATERIAL, &c.,

SMALL ENGINES, BOILERS, ELECTRIC MOTORS,

BATTERIES, DYNAMOS, &c., &c.

# Bailey's Patent Adjustable Planes.

**OVER 900,000 ALREADY SOLD.**

## Iron Planes.

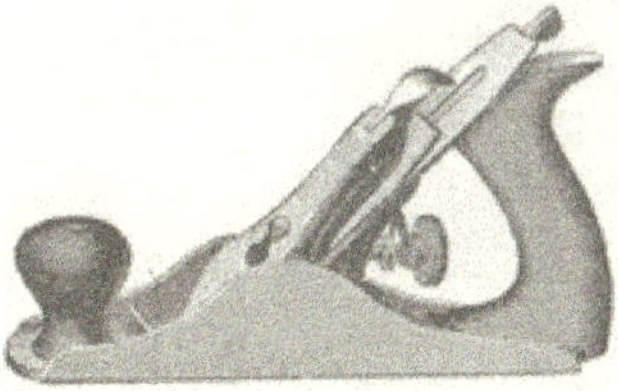

These Planes meet with universal approbation from the best Mechanics, as their extensive sale abundantly testifies. For beauty of style and finish, they are unequaled, and the superior methods for adjusting them readily in all their parts, render them economical to the owner.

| No. | | | | | | Each. |
|---|---|---|---|---|---|---|
| 1. | Smooth Plane, | 5½ | inches in Length, | 1¼ | inch Cutter.............. | $1.00 |
| 2. | Smooth Plane, | 7 | inches in Length, | 1⅝ | inch Cutter.............. | 1.25 |
| 3. | Smooth Plane, | 8 | inches in Length, | 1¾ | inch Cutter.............. | 1.35 |
| 4. | Smooth Plane, | 9 | inches in Length, | 2 | inch Cutter.............. | 1.45 |
| 4½. | Smooth Plane, | 10 | inches in Length, | 2⅜ | inch Cutter.............. | 1.70 |
| 5. | Jack Plane, | 14 | inches in Length, | 2 | inch Cutter.............. | 1.70 |
| 6. | Fore Plane, | 18 | inches in Length, | 2⅜ | inch Cutter.............. | 2.15 |
| 7. | Jointer Plane, | 22 | inches in Length, | 2⅜ | inch Cutter.............. | 2.45 |
| 8. | Jointer Plane, | 24 | inches in Length, | 2⅝ | inch Cutter.............. | 2.90 |
| 9. | Block Plane, | 10 | inches in Length, | 2 | inch Cutter.............. | 2.90 |

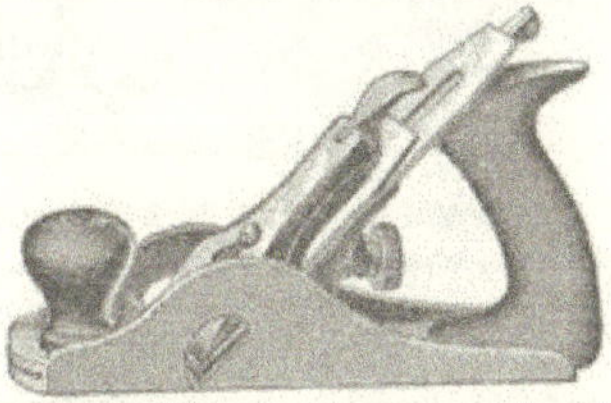

| | | |
|---|---|---|
| 10½. | Carriage Makers' Rabbet Plane, 9 inches Length, 2⅛ inch Cutter. | 1.70 |
| 10. | Carriage Makers' Rabbet Plane, 14 inches Length, 2⅛ inch Cutter. | 2.00 |
| 11. | Belt Makers' Plane, 2⅜ inch Cutter.............................. | 1.35 |

## Bailey's Adjustable Circular Plane.

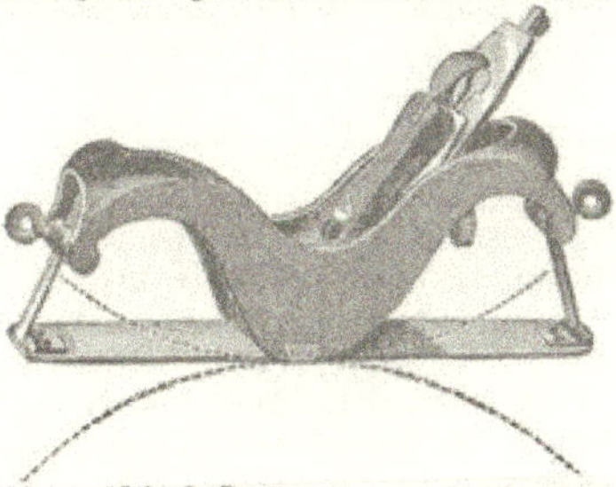

No. 13. Circular Plane, 1¾ inch Cutter................................ 1.80

**This Plane has a Flexible Steel Face, and by means of the thumb screws at each end of the Stock, can be easily adapted to plane circular work—either concave or convex.**

## Bailey's Adjustable Wood Planes.

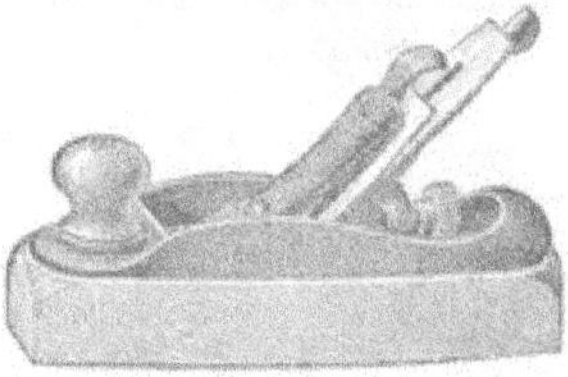

| No. | | Each. |
|---|---|---|
| 21. | Smooth Plane, 7 inches in Length, 1¾ inch Cutter................ | $0.90 |
| 22. | Smooth Plane, 8 inches in Length, 1¾ inch Cutter................ | .90 |
| 23. | Smooth Plane, 9 inches in Length, 1¾ inch Cutter................ | .90 |
| 24. | Smooth Plane, 8 inches in Length, 2 inch Cutter................ | .90 |
| 25. | Block Plane, 9½ inches in Length, 1¾ inch Cutter................ | .90 |

| | | |
|---|---|---|
| 35. | Handle Smooth, 9 inches in Length, 2 inch Cutter............. | 1.10 |
| 36. | Handle Smooth, 10 inches in Length, 2⅜ inch Cutter............. | 1.25 |
| 37. | Jenny Smooth, 13 inches in Length, 2⅝ inch Cutter............. | 1.35 |

| | | |
|---|---|---|
| 26. | Jack Plane, 15 inches in Length, 2 inch Cutter............... | 1.00 |
| 27. | Jack Plane, 15 inches in Length, 2⅛ inch Cutter............... | 1.13 |
| 28. | Fore Plane, 18 inches in Length, 2⅜ inch Cutter............... | 1.25 |
| 29. | Fore Plane, 20 inches in Length, 2⅜ inch Cutter............... | 1.25 |
| 30. | Jointer Plane, 22 inches in Length, 2⅜ inch Cutter............... | 1.35 |
| 31. | Jointer Plane, 24 inches in Length, 2⅜ inch Cutter............... | 1.35 |
| 32. | Jointer Plane, 26 inches in Length, 2⅝ inch Cutter............... | 1.45 |
| 33. | Jointer Plane, 28 inches in Length, 2⅝ inch Cutter............... | 1.45 |
| 34. | Jointer Plane, 30 inches in Length, 2⅝ inch Cutter............... | 1.55 |

## Stanley Iron Block Planes.

| No. | | Each. |
|---|---|---|
| 101. | Block Plane, 3½ inches in Length, 1 inch Cutter............... | $0.10 |

| | | |
|---|---|---|
| 102. | Block Plane, 5½ inches in Length, 1½ inch Cutter.............. | .20 |
| 103. | Block Plane, Adjustable, 5½ inches in Length, 1½ inch Cutter.... | .30 |

| | | |
|---|---|---|
| 110. | Block Plane, 7½ inches in Length, 1⅜ inch Cutter.............. | .30 |

| | | |
|---|---|---|
| 120. | Block Plane, Adjustable, 7½ inches in Length, 1¾ inch Cutter.... | .40 |

| | | |
|---|---|---|
| 130. | Block Plane (Double-Ender), 8 in. in Length, 1¾ in. Cutter...... | .40 |

This Plane has two slots, and two cutter seats. It can be used as a Block Plane, or, by reversing the position of the cutter and the clamping wedge (see dotted lines in the engraving) it can be used to plane close up into corners, or places difficult to reach with any other plane.

## Bull-Nose Rabbet Plane.

| No. | | Each. |
|---|---|---|
| 75. | Iron Stock, 4 inches in Length, 1 inch Cutter.................. | $0.25 |

# Augers and Bits.

German Pattern Gimlet Bits.......................................... 10 cts. each

## Clark's Extension Bits.

Small Size, Boring ½ to 1½.......................................... $1.15 each
Large    "      "    ⅞ to 3.......................................... 1.75  "

## Extra Cast Steel Auger Bits.

| Size, | ³⁄₁₆ | ¼ | ⁵⁄₁₆ | ⅜ | ⁷⁄₁₆ | ½ | ⁹⁄₁₆ | ⅝ | ¹¹⁄₁₆ | ¾ | ¹³⁄₁₆ | ⅞ | ¹⁵⁄₁₆ | 1 |
|---|---|---|---|---|---|---|---|---|---|---|---|---|---|---|
| Price, $ | .18 | .15 | .15 | .17 | .17 | .18 | .20 | .23 | .25 | .28 | .30 | .33 | .37 | .40 |

## Jenning's Pattern Auger Bits.

| Size, | ³⁄₁₆ | ¼ | ⁵⁄₁₆ | ⅜ | ⁷⁄₁₆ | ½ | ⁹⁄₁₆ | ⅝ | ¹¹⁄₁₆ | ¾ | ¹³⁄₁₆ | ⅞ | ¹⁵⁄₁₆ | 1 |
|---|---|---|---|---|---|---|---|---|---|---|---|---|---|---|
| Price, $ | .22 | .20 | .22 | .25 | .29 | .31 | .33 | .35 | .40 | .45 | .48 | .54 | .55 | .58 |

We keep in stock both styles of Auger Bits to 1½ by 16ths.

Also all sizes of

Hollow Augers,                     Carpenter's Augers,
Ship Augers,                       Nail Hammers,
Mill Augers,                       Bit Stocks,
Hatchets,                          Screws, Hinges. &c.

## No. 1. C. S. FIRMER CHISELS. The 1 inch is 5½ inches long from bolster to point.

BUCK BROS CAST STEEL BUCK BROTHERS

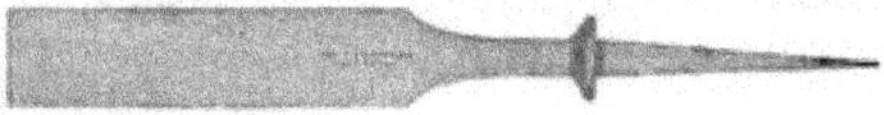

| 1/8 | 1/4 | 3/8 | 1/2 | 5/8 | 3/4 | 7/8 | 1 | 1 1/4 | 1 1/2 | 1 3/4 | 2 inches. | Set of 12 (one of each), $3.50. |
|---|---|---|---|---|---|---|---|---|---|---|---|---|
| $1.60 | 1.60 | 1.80 | 2.10 | 2.25 | 2.45 | 2.80 | 3.00 | 4.40 | 5.10 | 6.20 | 7.50 per dozen. | |

## No. 2. HANDLED FIRMER CHISELS. Sharp and Honed. The 1 in. is 5½ in. long from bolster to point.

BUCK BROS CAST STEEL BUCK BROTHERS

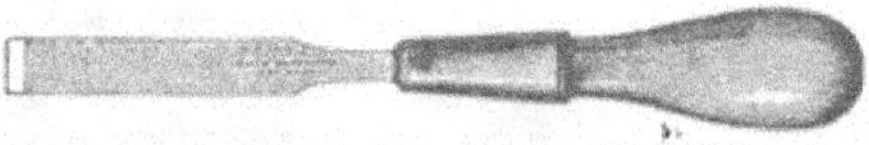

| 1/8 | 1/4 | 3/8 | 1/2 | 5/8 | 3/4 | 7/8 | 1 | 1 1/4 | 1 1/2 | 1 3/4 | 2 inches. | Set of 12 (one of each), $4.80. |
|---|---|---|---|---|---|---|---|---|---|---|---|---|
| $2.50 | 2.60 | 2.85 | 3.15 | 3.40 | 3.70 | 4.10 | 4.30 | 5.60 | 6.70 | 8.00 | 9.40 per dozen. | |

## No. 7. C. S. FIRMER GOUGES. Beveled Outside. The 1 inch is 5½ inches long from bolster to point.

BUCK BROS CAST STEEL BUCK BROTHERS

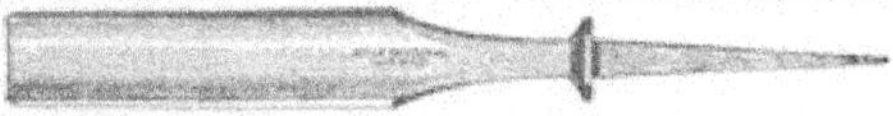

| 1/8 | 1/4 | 3/8 | 1/2 | 5/8 | 3/4 | 7/8 | 1 | 1 1/4 | 1 1/2 | 1 3/4 | 2 inches. | Set of 12 (one of each), $4.15. |
|---|---|---|---|---|---|---|---|---|---|---|---|---|
| $2.00 | 2.00 | 2.15 | 2.45 | 2.65 | 2.90 | 3.30 | 3.50 | 4.70 | 6.00 | 7.30 | 9.00 per dozen. | |

## No. 8. HANDLED FIRMER GOUGES. Beveled Outside. Sharp. The 1 in. is 5½ in. long from bolster.

BUCK BROS CAST STEEL BUCK BROTHERS

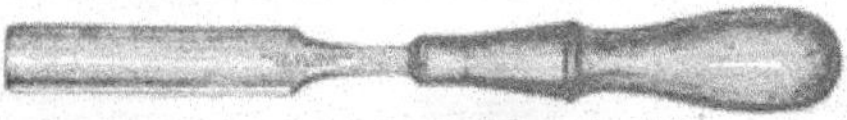

| 1/8 | 1/4 | 3/8 | 1/2 | 5/8 | 3/4 | 7/8 | 1 | 1 1/4 | 1 1/2 | 1 3/4 | 2 inches. | Set of 12 (one of each), $5.80. |
|---|---|---|---|---|---|---|---|---|---|---|---|---|
| $3.15 | 3.30 | 3.60 | 3.85 | 4.10 | 4.45 | 4.90 | 5.10 | 6.70 | 8.00 | 9.45 | 11.20 per dozen. | |

## No. 9. C. S. FIRMER GOUGES. Beveled Inside. The 1 in. is 5½ in. long from bolster to point.

BUCK BROS CAST STEEL BUCK BROTHERS

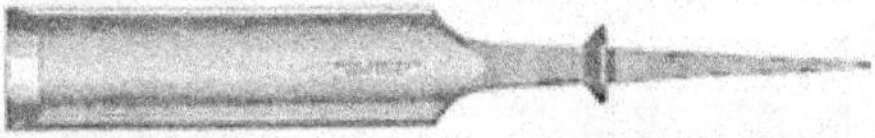

| 1/8 | 1/4 | 3/8 | 1/2 | 5/8 | 3/4 | 7/8 | 1 | 1 1/4 | 1 1/2 | 1 3/4 | 2 inches. | Set of 12 (one of each), $4.45. |
|---|---|---|---|---|---|---|---|---|---|---|---|---|
| $2.20 | 2.25 | 2.40 | 2.70 | 2.90 | 3.15 | 3.55 | 3.75 | 5.15 | 6.30 | 7.65 | 9.35 per dozen. | Regular, Middle and Flat Sweeps. |

## No. 10. HANDLED FIRMER GOUGES. Beveled Inside. Sharpened. The 1 in. is 5½ in. long from bolster.

BUCK BROS CAST STEEL BUCK BROTHERS

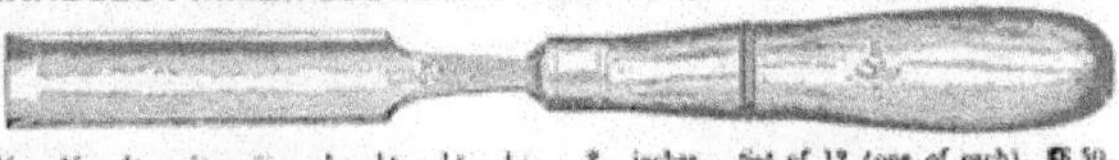

| 1/8 | 1/4 | 3/8 | 1/2 | 5/8 | 3/4 | 7/8 | 1 | 1 1/4 | 1 1/2 | 1 3/4 | 2 inches. | Set of 12 (one of each), $6.50. |
|---|---|---|---|---|---|---|---|---|---|---|---|---|
| $3.70 | 3.85 | 4.15 | 4.40 | 4.60 | 5.00 | 5.40 | 5.65 | 7.30 | 8.55 | 10.10 | 11.85 per dozen. | Regular, Middle and Flat Sweeps. |

## No. 11. C. S. PARING CHISELS. The 1 in. is 8½ in. long from bolster to point.

BUCK BROS CAST STEEL BUCK BROTHERS

| 1/8 | 1/4 | 3/8 | 1/2 | 5/8 | 3/4 | 7/8 | 1 | 1 1/4 | 1 1/2 | 1 3/4 | 2 inches. | Set of 12 (one of each), $5.50. |
|---|---|---|---|---|---|---|---|---|---|---|---|---|
| $2.80 | 2.80 | 2.90 | 3.20 | 3.55 | 4.00 | 4.30 | 5.25 | 7.15 | 8.60 | 10.15 | 12.50 per dozen. | |

## No. 12. HANDLED PARING CHISELS. Sharp and Honed. The 1 in. is 8½ in. long from bolster.

BUCK BROS CAST STEEL BUCK BROTHERS

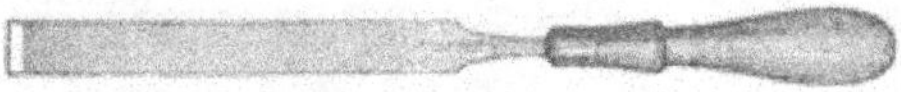

| 1/8 | 1/4 | 3/8 | 1/2 | 5/8 | 3/4 | 7/8 | 1 | 1 1/4 | 1 1/2 | 1 3/4 | 2 inches. | Set of 12 (one of each), $7.45. |
|---|---|---|---|---|---|---|---|---|---|---|---|---|
| $3.85 | 4.00 | 4.25 | 4.45 | 5.00 | 5.30 | 5.90 | 6.85 | 8.20 | 10.00 | 12.25 | 14.70 per dozen. | |

## No. 13. C. S. PARING GOUGES. Beveled Inside. The 1 in. is 8½ in. long from bolster.

BUCK BROS CAST STEEL BUCK BROTHERS

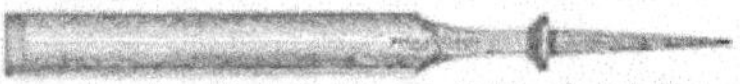

| 1/8 | 1/4 | 3/8 | 1/2 | 5/8 | 3/4 | 7/8 | 1 | 1 1/4 | 1 1/2 | 1 3/4 | 2 inches. | Set of 12 (one of each), $8.00. |
|---|---|---|---|---|---|---|---|---|---|---|---|---|
| $4.65 | 4.70 | 4.80 | 5.10 | 5.40 | 5.90 | 6.15 | 7.15 | 9.35 | 10.90 | 13.15 | 15.60 per dozen. | Regular, Middle and Flat Sweeps. |

## No. 14. HANDLED PARING GOUGES. Beveled Inside. Sharpened. The 1 in. is 8½ in. long from bolster.

BUCK BROS CAST STEEL BUCK BROTHERS

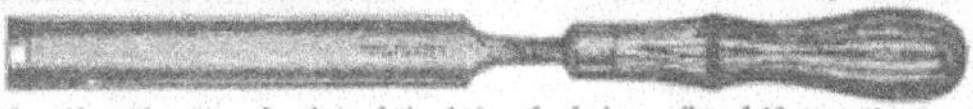

| 1/8 | 1/4 | 3/8 | 1/2 | 5/8 | 3/4 | 7/8 | 1 | 1 1/4 | 1 1/2 | 1 3/4 | 2 inches. | Set of 12 (one of each), $10.15. |
|---|---|---|---|---|---|---|---|---|---|---|---|---|
| $6.20 | 6.35 | 6.65 | 6.85 | 7.40 | 7.90 | 8.25 | 9.25 | 11.65 | 13.40 | 16.00 | 18.40 per dozen. | Regular, Middle and Flat Sweeps. |

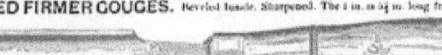

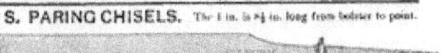

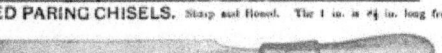

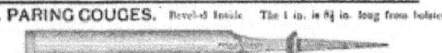

## No. 15. HANDLED PARING CHISELS. Best Shanks.

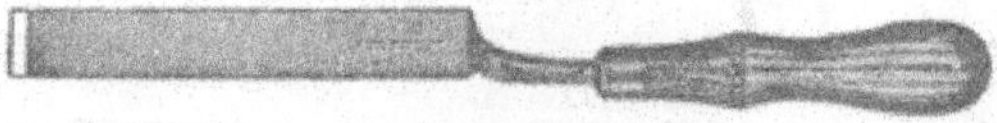

| ⅛ | ¼ | ⅜ | ½ | ⅝ | ¾ | ⅞ | 1 | 1¼ | 1½ | 1¾ | 2 inches. | |
|---|---|---|---|---|---|---|---|---|---|---|---|---|
| $5.25 | 5.65 | 6.00 | 6.30 | 7.20 | 7.90 | 8.50 | 10.00 | 12.90 | 15.35 | 18.06 | 21.60 per doz. | Set of 12 (one of each), $10.80. |

## C. S. TURNING CHISELS.

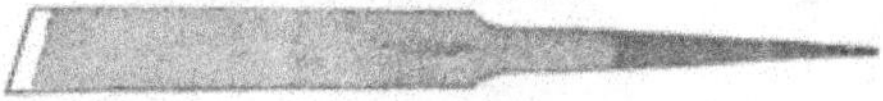

| | ⅛ | ¼ | ⅜ | ½ | ⅝ | ¾ | ⅞ | 1 | 1¼ | 1½ | 1¾ | 2 inches. | |
|---|---|---|---|---|---|---|---|---|---|---|---|---|---|
| No. 16. C. S. TURNING CHISELS. Regular. | $2.20 | 2.25 | 2.45 | 2.70 | 3.00 | 3.40 | 3.70 | 4.35 | 5.40 | 7.00 | 8.40 | 10.00 per dozen. | Set of 12 (one of each), $4.90. |
| No. 21. C. S. TURNING CHISELS. Extra Long. | $3.00 | 3.00 | 3.20 | 3.45 | 3.75 | 4.10 | 4.50 | 5.10 | 6.20 | 7.70 | 9.20 | 10.70 per dozen. | Set of 12 (one of each), $5.65. |
| No. 23. C. S. TURNING CHISELS. Long and Strong. | $4.10 | 4.15 | 4.30 | 4.50 | 4.85 | 5.40 | 5.80 | 6.75 | 8.25 | 10.50 | 13.50 | 16.75 per dozen. | Set of 12 (one of each), $7.75. |

The 1 inch No. 16 is 10½ inches long, the No. 21 is 11 inches long, and No. 23 is 13 inches long over all.

## C. S. TURNING GOUGES.

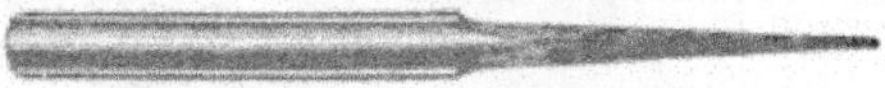

| | ⅛ | ¼ | ⅜ | ½ | ⅝ | ¾ | ⅞ | 1 | 1¼ | 1½ | 1¾ | 2 inches. | |
|---|---|---|---|---|---|---|---|---|---|---|---|---|---|
| No. 17. C. S. TURNING GOUGES. Regular. | $2.90 | 2.90 | 3.30 | 3.65 | 3.95 | 4.60 | 5.25 | 5.90 | 7.70 | 10.00 | 11.80 | 14.50 per dozen. | Set of 12 (one of each), $6.70. |
| No. 22. C. S. TURNING GOUGES. Extra Long. | $3.65 | 3.70 | 4.00 | 4.40 | 4.70 | 5.35 | 6.00 | 6.70 | 8.45 | 10.80 | 12.35 | 15.20 per dozen. | Set of 12 (one of each), $7.40. |
| No. 24. C. S. TURNING GOUGES. Long and Strong. | $5.70 | 5.80 | 6.00 | 7.00 | 7.70 | 8.75 | 10.10 | 11.10 | 13.50 | 16.90 | 18.75 | 21.50 per dozen. | Set of 12 (one of each), $11.40. |

The 1 inch No. 17 is 10½ inches long, the No. 22 is 11 inches long, and No. 24 is 13 inches long over all.

## No. 19. HANDLED TURNING CHISELS. Ground Sharp.

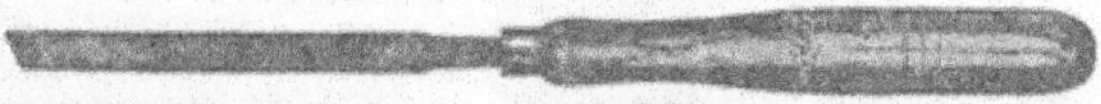

| ⅛ | ¼ | ⅜ | ½ | ⅝ | ¾ | ⅞ | 1 | 1¼ | 1½ | 1¾ | 2 inches. | |
|---|---|---|---|---|---|---|---|---|---|---|---|---|
| $4.15 | 4.25 | 4.50 | 5.00 | 5.40 | 6.00 | 6.70 | 7.60 | 8.75 | 10.75 | 13.00 | 16.00 per dozen. | Set of 12 (one of each), $7.85. |

## No. 20. HANDLED TURNING GOUGES. Ground Sharp.

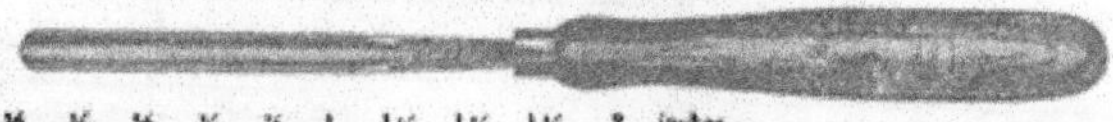

| ⅛ | ¼ | ⅜ | ½ | ⅝ | ¾ | ⅞ | 1 | 1¼ | 1½ | 1¾ | 2 inches. | |
|---|---|---|---|---|---|---|---|---|---|---|---|---|
| $5.35 | 5.50 | 5.65 | 6.25 | 6.65 | 7.50 | 8.55 | 9.45 | 11.35 | 14.10 | 17.00 | 21.50 per dozen. | Set of 12 (one of each), $10.25. |

## No. 18. WOOD TURNERS' PARTING OR CUTTING OFF TOOLS.

The ⅛ inch wide measures 6½ inches over all.

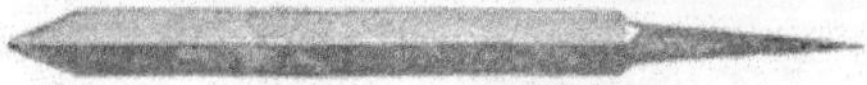

| ⅛ | 3/16 | ¼ inch. |
|---|---|---|
| $4.50 | 5.00 | 5.50 per dozen. |

## No. 25. WOOD TURNERS' SIZING TOOLS.

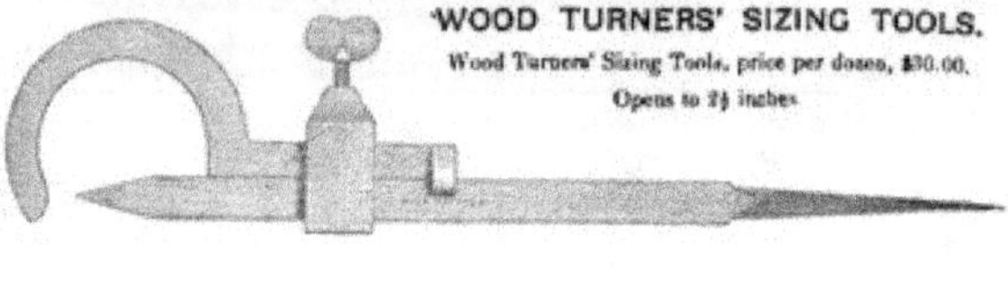

Wood Turners' Sizing Tools, price per dozen, $30.00.

Opens to 2½ inches.

## No. 28. C. S. FIRMER CHISELS.

Beveled Edges. The 1 inch is 5¼ inches long from bolster to point.

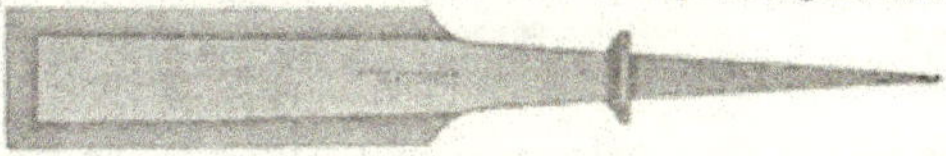

| ⅛ | ¼ | ⅜ | ½ | ⅝ | ¾ | ⅞ | 1 | 1¼ | 1½ | 1¾ | 2 | inches. |
|---|---|---|---|---|---|---|---|---|---|---|---|---|
| $3.80 | 3.85 | 4.00 | 4.40 | 4.60 | 4.75 | 5.00 | 5.40 | 7.15 | 8.25 | 10.40 | 12.00 | per dozen. |

Set of 12 (one of each), $8.40.

## No. 30. HANDLED FIRMER CHISELS.

Beveled Edges. The 1 inch is 5¼ inches long from bolster.

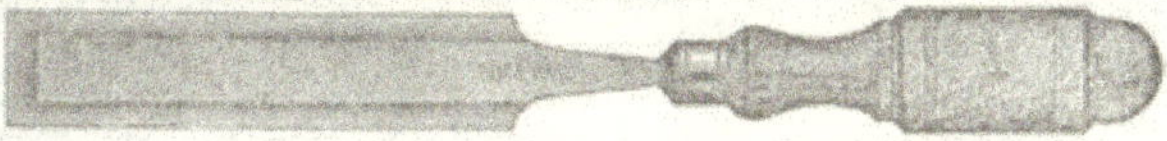

| ⅛ | ¼ | ⅜ | ½ | ⅝ | ¾ | ⅞ | 1 | 1¼ | 1½ | 1¾ | 2 | inches. |
|---|---|---|---|---|---|---|---|---|---|---|---|---|
| $4.70 | 4.85 | 5.10 | 5.45 | 5.80 | 6.05 | 6.25 | 6.70 | 8.75 | 9.90 | 12.65 | 13.90 | per dozen. |

Ground Sharp and Honed. Set of 12 (one of each), $7.75.

## No. 31. C. S. PARING CHISELS.

Beveled Edges. The 1 inch is 8½ inches long from bolster to point.

| ⅛ | ¼ | ⅜ | ½ | ⅝ | ¾ | ⅞ | 1 | 1¼ | 1½ | 1¾ | 2 | inches. |
|---|---|---|---|---|---|---|---|---|---|---|---|---|
| $5.75 | 5.90 | 6.00 | 6.15 | 6.50 | 6.90 | 7.20 | 8.50 | 10.90 | 12.40 | 14.80 | 17.40 | per dozen. |

Set of 12 (one of each), $9.50.

## No. 32. HANDLED PARING CHISELS.

Beveled Edges. The 1 in. is 8½ in. long from bolster to point.

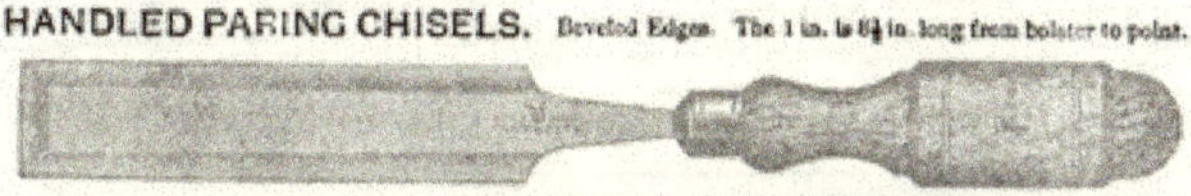

| ⅛ | ¼ | ⅜ | ½ | ⅝ | ¾ | ⅞ | 1 | 1¼ | 1½ | 1¾ | 2 | inches. |
|---|---|---|---|---|---|---|---|---|---|---|---|---|
| $7.20 | 7.20 | 7.35 | 7.50 | 8.10 | 8.50 | 8.90 | 9.85 | 12.70 | 14.50 | 17.10 | 19.65 | per dozen. |

Set of 12 (one of each), $11.25. Sharp and Honed.

## No. 33. STANDARD EXTRA SOCKET FIRMER CHISELS.

The 1 inch is 6 inches long in the blade.

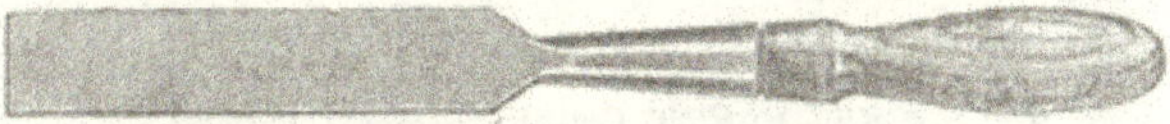

| ⅛ | ¼ | ⅜ | ½ | ⅝ | ¾ | ⅞ | 1 | 1¼ | 1½ | 1¾ | 2 | inches. |
|---|---|---|---|---|---|---|---|---|---|---|---|---|
| $4.00 | 4.20 | 4.30 | 4.80 | 5.25 | 5.60 | 6.25 | 6.60 | 7.40 | 8.20 | 9.00 | 10.00 | per dozen. |

Set of 12 (one of each), $6.00.

## No. 34. STANDARD EXTRA SOCKET FIRMER CHISELS.

Beveled Edges. The 1 inch is 6 inches long in the blade.

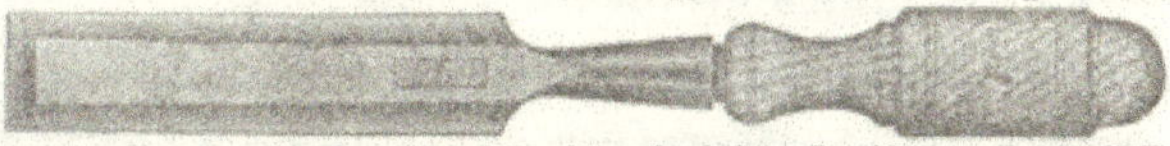

| ⅛ | ¼ | ⅜ | ½ | ⅝ | ¾ | ⅞ | 1 | 1¼ | 1½ | 1¾ | 2 | inches. |
|---|---|---|---|---|---|---|---|---|---|---|---|---|
| $6.35 | 6.55 | 6.80 | 7.25 | 7.65 | 8.10 | 8.70 | 9.25 | 10.70 | 11.50 | 13.40 | 14.60 | per dozen. |

Set of 12 (one of each), $9.25.

## No. 35. No. 1 SOCKET FIRMER CHISELS.

The 1 inch is 5¼ inches long in the blade.

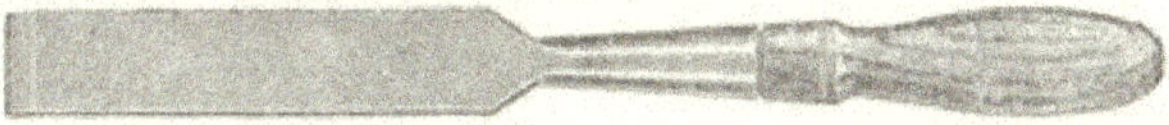

| ⅛ | ¼ | ⅜ | ½ | ⅝ | ¾ | ⅞ | 1 | 1¼ | 1½ | 1¾ | 2 | inches. |
|---|---|---|---|---|---|---|---|---|---|---|---|---|
| $3.75 | 3.90 | 4.15 | 4.40 | 4.85 | 5.25 | 5.60 | 6.10 | 6.75 | 7.35 | 8.25 | 9.20 | per dozen. |

Set of 12 (one of each), $5.40.

## No. 36. No. 1 SOCKET FIRMER CHISELS.

Beveled Edges. The 1 in. is 5¼ in. long in the blade.

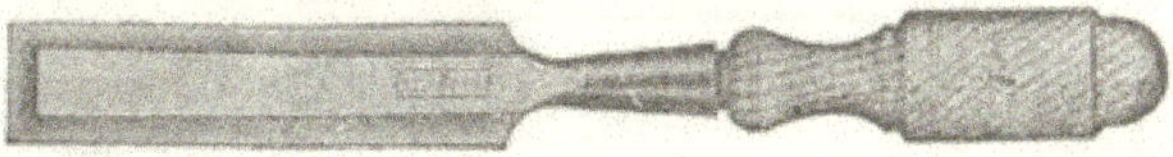

| ⅛ | ¼ | ⅜ | ½ | ⅝ | ¾ | ⅞ | 1 | 1¼ | 1½ | 1¾ | 2 | inches. |
|---|---|---|---|---|---|---|---|---|---|---|---|---|
| $6.00 | 6.15 | 6.40 | 6.80 | 7.20 | 7.75 | 8.10 | 8.60 | 9.90 | 10.65 | 12.50 | 13.80 | per dozen. |

Set of 12 (one of each), $8.65.

## No. 40. EXTRA SOCKET FIRMER GOUGES. Beveled Outside. The 1 in. is 6 in. long in the blade.

BUCK BROS CAST STEEL BUCK BROTHERS

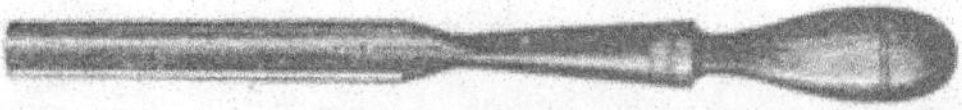

| | | | | | | | | | | | | |
|---|---|---|---|---|---|---|---|---|---|---|---|---|
| ⅛ | ¼ | ⅜ | ½ | ⅝ | ¾ | ⅞ | 1 | 1¼ | 1½ | 1¾ | 2 | inches. Set of 12 (one of each), $8.20. |
| $5.20 | 5.50 | 5.90 | 6.30 | 6.75 | 7.40 | 8.10 | 8.50 | 9.50 | 10.60 | 11.65 | 13.15 | per dozen. Regular Sweep. |

## No. 41. EXTRA SOCKET FIRMER GOUGES. Beveled Inside. The 1 in. is 6 in. long in the blade.

BUCK BROS CAST STEEL BUCK BROTHERS

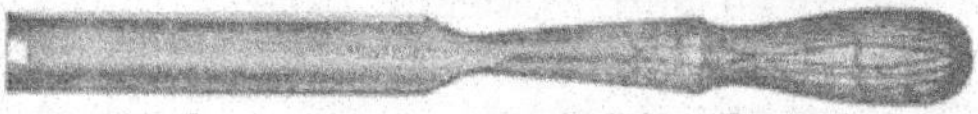

| | | | | | | | | | | | | |
|---|---|---|---|---|---|---|---|---|---|---|---|---|
| ⅛ | ¼ | ⅜ | ½ | ⅝ | ¾ | ⅞ | 1 | 1¼ | 1½ | 1¾ | 2 | inches. Set of 12 (one of each), $8.75. |
| $5.55 | 5.95 | 6.35 | 6.75 | 7.15 | 7.75 | 8.55 | 8.95 | 10.05 | 11.15 | 12.30 | 13.80 | per doz. Regular, Middle and Flat Sweeps. |

## No. 42. No. 1 SOCKET FIRMER GOUGES. Beveled Outside. The 1 in. is 5½ in. long in the blade.

BUCK BROS CAST STEEL BUCK BROTHERS

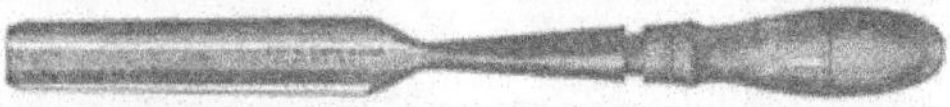

| | | | | | | | | | | | | |
|---|---|---|---|---|---|---|---|---|---|---|---|---|
| ⅛ | ¼ | ⅜ | ½ | ⅝ | ¾ | ⅞ | 1 | 1¼ | 1½ | 1¾ | 2 | inches. Set of 12 (one of each), $7.25. |
| $4.60 | 5.00 | 5.35 | 5.60 | 5.80 | 6.40 | 7.00 | 7.50 | 8.40 | 9.20 | 10.25 | 11.40 | per dozen. Regular Sweep. |

## No. 43. SOCKET PARING CHISELS. All sizes 8 inches long in the blade.

BUCK BROS CAST STEEL BUCK BROTHERS

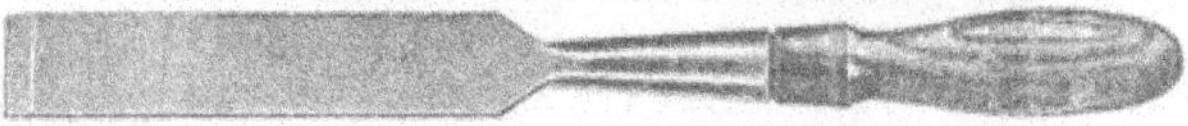

| | | | | | | | | | | | | |
|---|---|---|---|---|---|---|---|---|---|---|---|---|
| ⅛ | ¼ | ⅜ | ½ | ⅝ | ¾ | ⅞ | 1 | 1¼ | 1½ | 1¾ | 2 | inches. Set of 12 (one of each), $8.75. |
| $5.80 | 5.85 | 6.25 | 6.75 | 7.40 | 8.25 | 8.70 | 9.20 | 10.35 | 11.25 | 12.40 | 14.00 | per dozen. |

## No. 44. SOCKET PARING CHISELS. Beveled Edges. All sizes 8 inches long in the blade.

BUCK BROS CAST STEEL BUCK BROTHERS

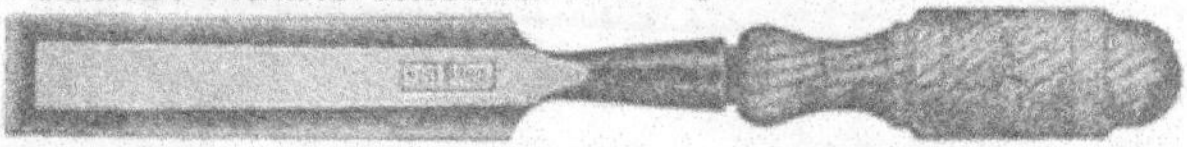

| | | | | | | | | | | | | |
|---|---|---|---|---|---|---|---|---|---|---|---|---|
| ⅛ | ¼ | ⅜ | ½ | ⅝ | ¾ | ⅞ | 1 | 1¼ | 1½ | 1¾ | 2 | inches. Set of 12 (one of each), $12.50 |
| $8.10 | 8.35 | 8.75 | 9.25 | 10.00 | 10.80 | 11.45 | 12.10 | 13.90 | 15.20 | 17.10 | 19.00 | per dozen |

## No. 45. SOCKET PARING CHISELS. All sizes 10 inches long in the blade.

BUCK BROS CAST STEEL BUCK BROTHERS

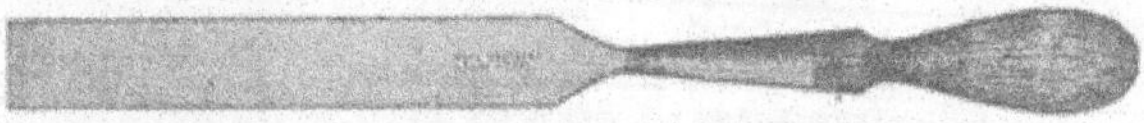

| | | | | | | | | | | | | |
|---|---|---|---|---|---|---|---|---|---|---|---|---|
| ⅛ | ¼ | ⅜ | ½ | ⅝ | ¾ | ⅞ | 1 | 1¼ | 1½ | 1¾ | 2 | inches. Set of 12 (one of each), $12.[illegible] |
| $7.50 | 7.70 | 8.25 | 8.75 | 9.80 | 10.80 | 12.00 | 13.00 | 14.30 | 16.00 | 17.50 | 19.00 | per dozen. |

## No. 46. SOCKET PARING GOUGES. Beveled Inside. All sizes 8 inches long in the blade

BUCK BROS CAST STEEL BUCK BROTHERS

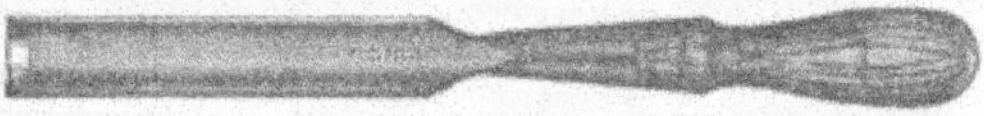

| | | | | | | | | | | | | |
|---|---|---|---|---|---|---|---|---|---|---|---|---|
| ⅛ | ¼ | ⅜ | ½ | ⅝ | ¾ | ⅞ | 1 | 1¼ | 1½ | 1¾ | 2 | inches. Set of 12 (one of each), $11.50. |
| $7.00 | 7.25 | 8.00 | 8.75 | 9.50 | 10.40 | 11.00 | 12.00 | 13.50 | 15.00 | 16.00 | 17.40 | per doz. Regular, Middle and Flat Sweeps. |

## No. 47. COACH MAKERS' SOCKET FIRMER CHISELS.

The 1 inch is 6¾ inches long in the blade.

BUCK BROS CAST STEEL BUCK BROTHERS

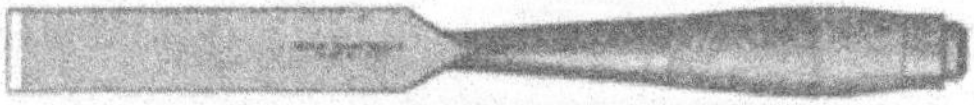

| | | | | | | | | | | | | |
|---|---|---|---|---|---|---|---|---|---|---|---|---|
| ⅛ | ¼ | ⅜ | ½ | ⅝ | ¾ | ⅞ | 1 | 1¼ | 1½ | 1¾ | 2 | inches. Set of 12 (one of each), $9.10, |
| $7.00 | 7.40 | 7.70 | 8.10 | 8.50 | 9.25 | 10.00 | 10.70 | 11.25 | 12.00 | 13.00 | 14.00 | per dozen. |

## No. 48. SOCKET MORTISE CHISELS. The ⅜ inch is 6¾ inches long in the blade.

BUCK BROS CAST STEEL BUCK BROTHERS

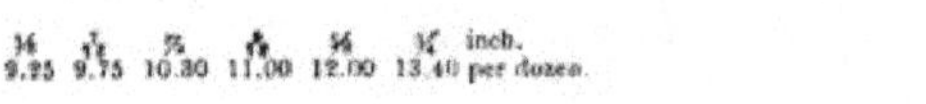

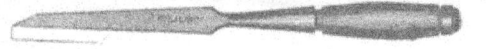

| | | | | | | | | | | |
|---|---|---|---|---|---|---|---|---|---|---|
| ⅛ | 3/16 | ¼ | 5/16 | ⅜ | 7/16 | ½ | 9/16 | ⅝ | ¾ | inch. |
| $7.50 | 8.00 | 8.50 | 8.80 | 9.25 | 9.75 | 10.30 | 11.00 | 12.00 | 13.40 | per dozen. |

## MILLWRIGHTS' SOCKET FIRMER CHISELS.

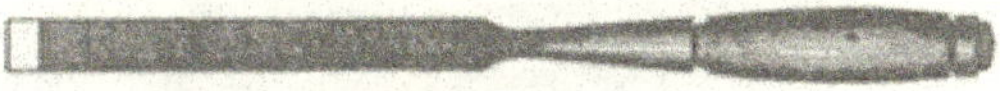

| ⅛ | ¼ | ⅜ | ½ | ⅝ | ¾ | ⅞ | 1 | 1¼ | 1½ | 1¾ | 2 | inches. | |
|---|---|---|---|---|---|---|---|---|---|---|---|---|---|
| **No. 49. BLADES 8 INCHES LONG. Solid Cast Steel.** | | | | | | | | | | | | | |
| $ 8.30 | 8.60 | 9.00 | 9.75 | 10.70 | 11.60 | 12.60 | 13.40 | 14.75 | 16.00 | 17.50 | 19.50 | per doz. | Set of 12 (one of each), $12.25. |
| **No. 50. BLADES 10 INCHES LONG. Solid Cast Steel.** | | | | | | | | | | | | | |
| $11.25 | 11.50 | 12.00 | 12.50 | 13.25 | 14.00 | 14.75 | 15.50 | 18.00 | 19.60 | 22.00 | 25.00 | per doz. | Set of 12 (one of each), $15.50. |
| **No. 51. BLADES 12 INCHES LONG. Solid Cast Steel.** | | | | | | | | | | | | | |
| $13.25 | 13.75 | 14.25 | 14.60 | 15.50 | 16.50 | 18.00 | 19.00 | 21.00 | 23.00 | 26.00 | 29.00 | per doz. | Set of 12 (one of each), $18.40. |

## No. 52. SOCKET DECK, OR SHIP-CARPENTERS' CHISELS.

5 to 6 inch blades, Solid Cast Steel.

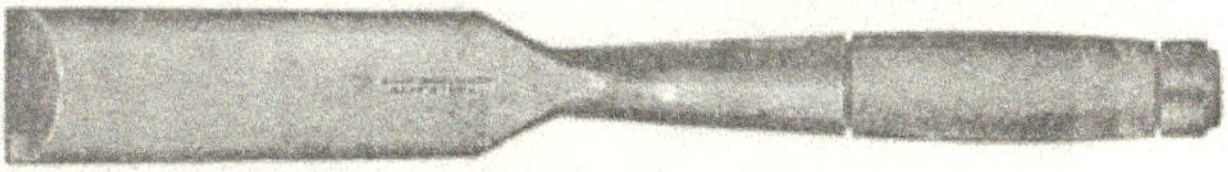

| 1 | 1¼ | 1½ | 2 | inches. |
|---|---|---|---|---|
| $10.50 | 11.25 | 12.00 | 13.50 | per dozen. |

## No. 53. CARPENTERS' SLICKS.

The 3 inch wide measures 10 inches long in the blade.

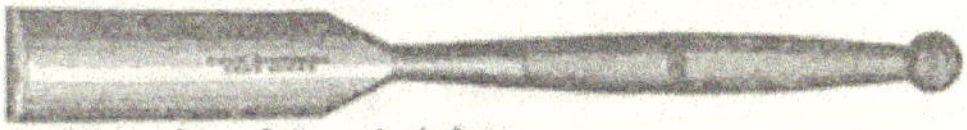

| 2½ | 3 | 3½ | 4 | inches. |
|---|---|---|---|---|
| $21.00 | 23.50 | 27.50 | 32.00 | per dozen. |

## MILLWRIGHTS' SOCKET FIRMER GOUGES.

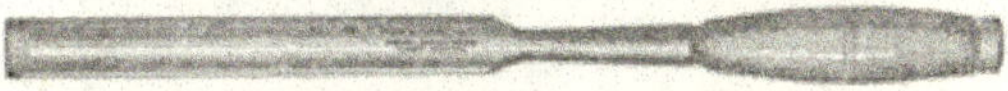

| ⅛ | ¼ | ⅜ | ½ | ⅝ | ¾ | ⅞ | 1 | 1¼ | 1½ | 1¾ | 2 | inches. | |
|---|---|---|---|---|---|---|---|---|---|---|---|---|---|
| **No. 54. BLADES 8 INCHES LONG. Solid Cast Steel.** | | | | | | | | | | | | | |
| $10.50 | 11.00 | 11.50 | 12.25 | 13.50 | 14.40 | 15.50 | 16.75 | 18.00 | 20.00 | 22.25 | 24.50 | per doz. | Set of 12 (one of each), $16.00. |
| **No. 55. BLADES 10 INCHES LONG. Solid Cast Steel.** | | | | | | | | | | | | | |
| $14.00 | 14.30 | 15.25 | 16.25 | 17.25 | 19.00 | 20.50 | 22.00 | 23.70 | 26.50 | 28.50 | 31.00 | per doz. | Set of 12 (one of each), $21.00. |

## No. 56. SOCKET FRAMING CHISELS.

7 to 8 inch blades.

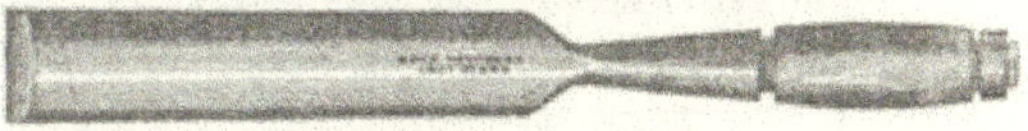

| ¼ | 5/16 | ⅜ | ½ | ⅝ | ¾ | ⅞ | 1 | 1¼ | 1½ | 1¾ | 2 | inches. | |
|---|---|---|---|---|---|---|---|---|---|---|---|---|---|
| $6.00 | 6.25 | 6.40 | 6.60 | 6.75 | 7.25 | 7.50 | 8.00 | 9.00 | 10.00 | 11.00 | 12.00 | per doz. | Set of 12 (one of each), $7.75. |

## No. 57. SOCKET CORNER CHISELS.

8 inch blades.

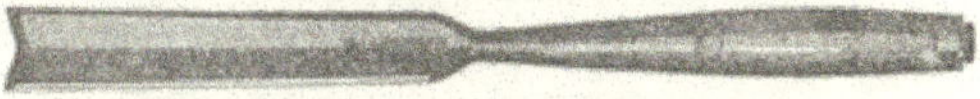

| ¾ | ⅞ | 1 | 1¼ | 1½ | inches. |
|---|---|---|---|---|---|
| $16.00 | 17.00 | 18.25 | 19.00 | 20.25 | per dozen. |

## No. 59. C. S. CUT PLANE IRONS.

| 1¼ | 1⅜ | 1½ | 1⅝ | 1¾ | 1⅞ | 2 | 2⅛ | 2¼ | 2⅜ | 2½ | 2⅝ | 2¾ | 2⅞ | 3 | inches. |
|---|---|---|---|---|---|---|---|---|---|---|---|---|---|---|---|
| $3.10 | 3.15 | 3.15 | 3.20 | 3.30 | 3.60 | 3.75 | 3.90 | 4.50 | 5.00 | 5.25 | 5.90 | 6.70 | 7.75 | 8.50 | per dozen. |

## No. 60. C. S. DOUBLE PLANE IRONS.

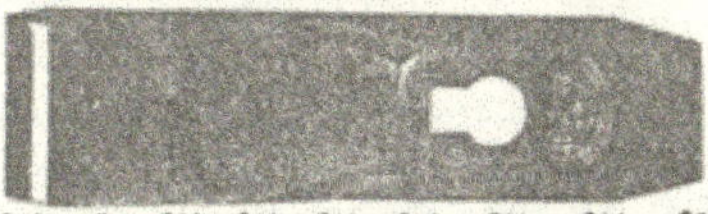

| 1¼ | 1⅜ | 1½ | 1⅝ | 1¾ | 1⅞ | 2 | 2⅛ | 2¼ | 2⅜ | 2½ | 2⅝ | 2¾ | 2⅞ | 3 | inches. |
|---|---|---|---|---|---|---|---|---|---|---|---|---|---|---|---|
| $6.00 | 6.00 | 6.10 | 6.10 | 6.30 | 6.70 | 6.90 | 7.20 | 7.90 | 8.75 | 9.30 | 10.15 | 11.15 | 13.00 | 14.20 | per dozen. |

## No. 63. C. S. TOOTH PLANE IRONS.

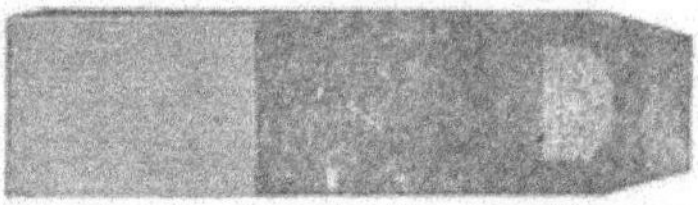

| | | | | | | | | | | | |
|---|---|---|---|---|---|---|---|---|---|---|---|
| 1⅜ | 1¼ | 1½ | 1⅝ | 1¾ | 1⅞ | 2 | 2⅛ | 2¼ | 2⅜ | 2½ | inches. |
| $4.50 | 4 50 | 4.50 | 4.50 | 4 50 | 4 90 | 5 25 | 5 60 | 6 10 | 6 40 | 6.85 | per dozen. |

We keep in stock three cuts of Tooth Irons, viz Fine, Medium and Coarse.

---

## No. 72. C. S. SCREW DRIVER BITTS.

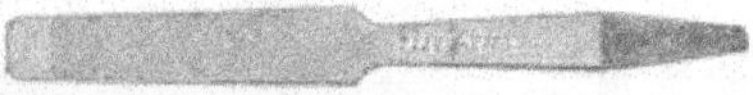

Length over all, 5 inches. Assorted Sizes Price per dozen, $1 90.

---

## No. 73. EXTRA LONG AND HEAVY C. S. SCREW DRIVER BITTS.

Length over all, 7 inches Assorted Sizes. Price per dozen, $2 65

---

## BEST QUALITY NAIL SETS.

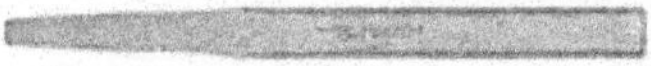

No. 76. Best Quality Square Point Nail Sets. Made in five sizes, being the size of Best English Cast Steel in the bar, viz 1/16, 1/32, 1/8, 3/32, 5/32 Square. Each Nail Set is stamped BUCK BROTHERS. They are tempered at both ends and are finished in the best style.
We send them assorted sizes unless otherwise ordered. Packed in ¼ Gross boxes with six round points in each box

Best Quality Nail Sets, assorted sizes, per gross, $16.00.

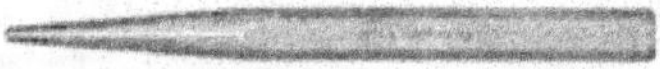

No. 77. Best Quality Round Point Nail Sets Made in five sizes, being the size of Best English Cast Steel in the bar, viz 1/16, 1/32, 1/8, 3/32, 5/32 Square. Each Nail Set is stamped BUCK BROTHERS They are tempered at both ends and are finished in the best style.
We send them assorted sizes unless otherwise ordered Packed in ¼ Gross boxes.

Best Quality Nail Sets, assorted sizes, per gross, $16 00.

---

## No. 80. BEST C. S. SQUARE REAMERS.

C. S Square Reamers, superior quality, per dozen, $2.35.
C. S. Flat Reamers, superior quality, per dozen, $2.35

---

## No. 81. BEST C. S. OCTAGON REAMERS.

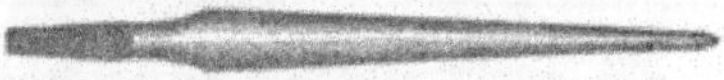

C. S. Half Round Reamers, superior quality, per dozen, $2.60.
C. S. Hexagon or Octagon Reamers, superior quality, per dozen, $2.75.

---

## No 82. C. S. FLAT COUNTERSINKS.

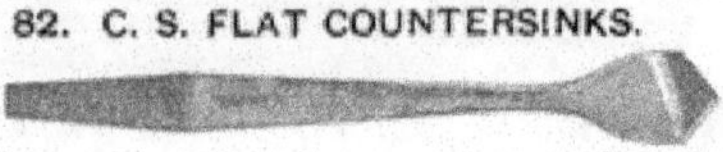

C. S. Flat Countersinks, superior quality, for iron, assorted sizes, per dozen, $2.50.

---

## No. 83. C. S. ROSE COUNTERSINKS.

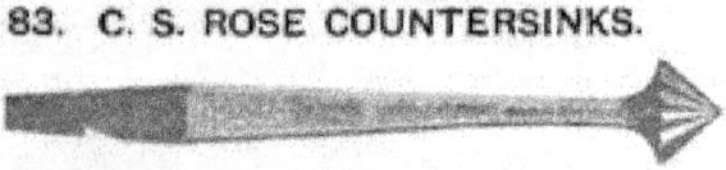

C. S. Rose Countersinks, superior quality, assorted sizes, per dozen, $2.75.
Extra Large Sizes will be charged extra prices.

## No. 84. C. S. SNAIL COUNTERSINKS.

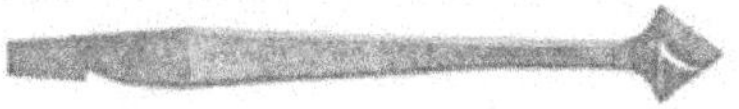

C. S. Snail Countersinks, superior quality, for wood, assorted sizes, per dozen, $2.50.
Extra Large Sizes will be charged extra prices.

## No. 85. BEST C. S. COLD CHISELS.

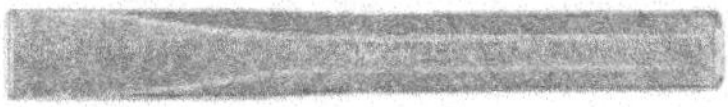

| ¼ | 5/16 | ⅜ | 7/16 | ½ | 9/16 | ⅝ | 11/16 | ¾ | ⅞ | 1 | inch |
|---|---|---|---|---|---|---|---|---|---|---|---|
| $2.00 | 2.00 | 2.40 | 2.75 | 3.00 | 3.50 | 4.00 | 4.50 | 5.25 | 7.50 | 11.00 | per dozen |

## No. 86. C. S. SCRATCH AWLS.

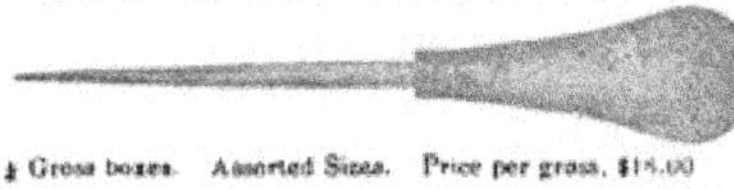

Packed in ½ Gross boxes. Assorted Sizes. Price per gross, $18.00

## PUNCHES.

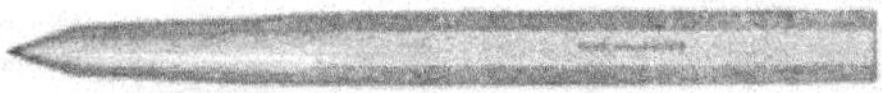

### No. 87. MACHINISTS' CENTRE PUNCHES.

| ⅜ | 7/16 | ½ inch. |
|---|---|---|
| $2.10 | $2.40 | $2.75 per dozen. |

Assorted sizes, 1 dozen in a box, $2.40 per dozen.

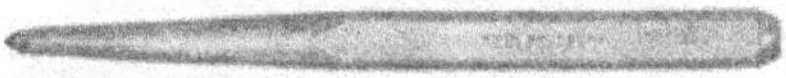

### No. 88. BRIGHT PRICK PUNCHES.

| ¼ | 5/16 | ⅜ inch |
|---|---|---|
| $1.75 | $1.90 | $2.20 per dozen |

Assorted sizes, 1 dozen in a box, $1.95 per dozen

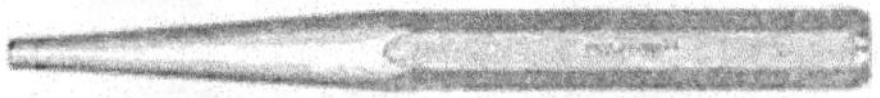

### No. 89. TINNERS' OR COOPERS' SOLID PUNCHES.

| ⅜ | 7/16 | ½ inch |
|---|---|---|
| $2.10. | $2.40 | $2.75 per dozen. |

Assorted sizes, 1 dozen in a box, $2.40 per dozen

### No. 90. BRIGHT SOLID PUNCHES.

| ¼ | 5/16 | ⅜ inch. |
|---|---|---|
| $1.75 | $1.90 | $2.20 per dozen. |

Assorted sizes, 1 dozen in a box, $1.95 per dozen.

## No. 91. CABINET MAKERS' BURNISHERS.

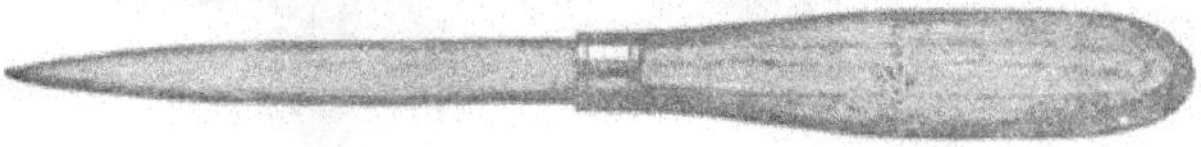

| 4 | 4½ | 5 | 6 inches. |
|---|---|---|---|
| $5.00 | $5.75 | $6.75 | $8.00 per dozen. |

| | | | |
|---|---|---|---|
| Assorted, 3 to 4 | inches, | . | 4.50 per dozen. |
| " 3 to 4½ | " | . | 5.00 " " |
| " 3 to 5 | " | . | 5.50 " " |
| " 3 to 6 | " | . | 6.25 " " |

# LONDON STYLE CARVING CHISELS AND GOUGES.

## HAND FORGED FROM BEST ENGLISH CAST STEEL.

| No. | CARVING CHISELS. | No. | FRONT BENT GOUGES. |
|---|---|---|---|

**CARVING CHISELS.**

1

**SKEW CARVING CHISELS.**

2

**STRAIGHT GOUGES.**

3
4
5
6
7
8
9
10
11

**CURVED GOUGES.**

12
13
14
15
16
17
18
19
20

**FRONT BENT CHISELS.**

21

**RIGHT CORNER.**

22

**LEFT CORNER.**

23

**FRONT BENT GOUGES.**

24
25
26
27
28
29
30
31
32

**BACK BENT GOUGES.**

33
34
35
36
37
38

**PARTING TOOLS.**

39
40
41
42
43
44
45
46

Parting Tools are measured the broadest way.

## Round Screw Drivers.

| Length of Blade, inch. | 1½ | 2 | 3 | 4 | 5 | 6 | 7 | 8 | 10 | 12 |
|---|---|---|---|---|---|---|---|---|---|---|
| Price, each, | $ .12 | .15 | .17 | .19 | .21 | .23 | .25 | .28 | .35 | .45 |

## Flat Screw Drivers.

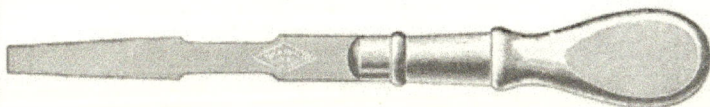

| Length of Blade. inch. | 2 | 3 | 4 | 5 | 6 | 7 | 8 | 10 | 12 |
|---|---|---|---|---|---|---|---|---|---|
| Price, each, | $ .20 | .23 | .26 | .33 | .40 | .52 | .65 | .90 | 1.15 |

## Ratchet Screw Driver.

A very convenient tool, it can be made to work either right or left by moving the button from one side to the other

| Length of Blade, inch, | 4 | 5 | 6 |
|---|---|---|---|
| Price, each, | $ .75 | .85 | 1.00 |

## The Ellis Water Filter.

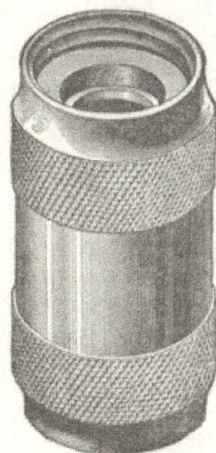

It is no longer considered safe to use water through a faucet for drinking or cooking purposes without being filtered. Conceding this fact, we must admit that the most simple, the most durable, and the cheapest (if it does the work as well or better), must be the most desirable.

One great objection to filters has been complication, it requiring a good mechanic to take apart, refill, and adjust properly. If in use a filter should be reversed as often as once a day.

In the Ellis, the best judges consider all objections overcome. It can be reversed by a child. It can be taken apart, refilled, and adjusted by any servant girl.

**PRICE, 75 CENTS EACH.**

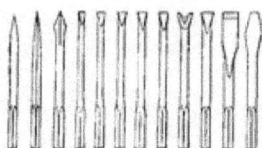

# BRASS THUMB SCREWS.

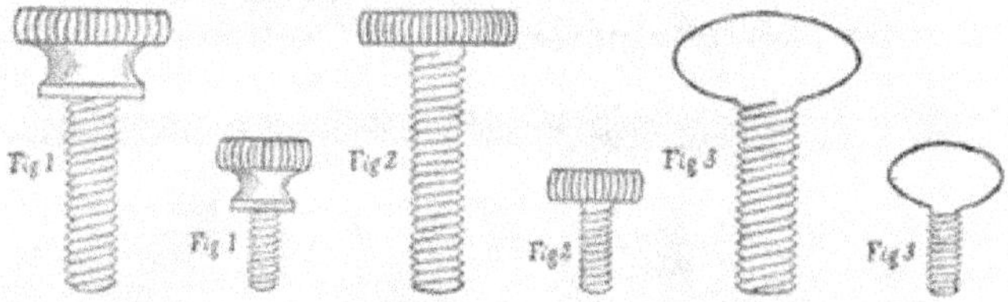
Fig 1
Fig 1
Fig 2
Fig 2
Fig 3
Fig 3

## BRASS THUMB NUTS. BRASS THUMB NUT BOLTS.

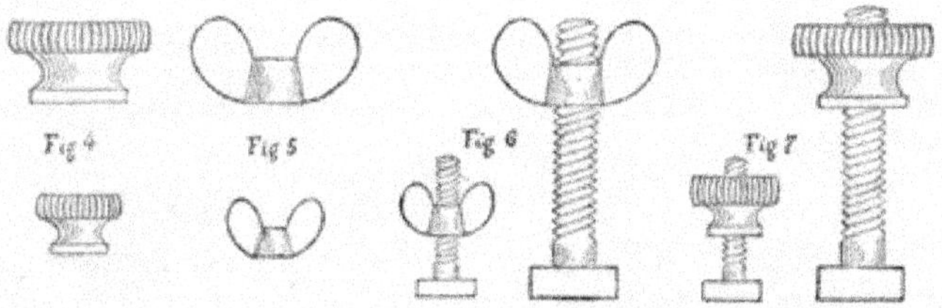
Fig 4
Fig 5
Fig 6
Fig 7

**Fig. 1. Brass Thumb Screws, WITH SHOULDER.**

| Size of Screw, | No. 4 | 8 | 12 |
|---|---|---|---|
| Threads to inch, | 36 | 32 | 24 |
| Length, inch, | 3/8 | 1/2 | 3/4 |
| Price per Doz. | .50 | .75 | 1.12 |
| Price each | .06 | .08 | .10 |

**Fig. 2. Brass Thumb Screws, PLAIN.**

| Size of Screw, | No. 4 | 8 | 12 |
|---|---|---|---|
| Threads to inch, | 36 | 32 | 24 |
| Length, inch, | 3/8 | 1/2 | 3/4 |
| Price per Doz. | .35 | .60 | .85 |
| Price, each, | .05 | .06 | .08 |

**Fig. 3. Flat Head Brass Thumb Screws.**

| Size of Screws, | No. 8 | 8 | 10 | 10 | 10 | 14 | 14 | 14 | 14 |
|---|---|---|---|---|---|---|---|---|---|
| Threads to inch, | 32 | 32 | 24 | 24 | 24 | 20 | 20 | 20 | 20 |
| Length, inch, | 3/8 | 1/2 | 1/2 | 3/4 | 1 | 1/2 | 3/4 | 1 | 1 1/2 |
| Price per Doz. | .30 | .30 | .35 | .40 | .45 | .45 | .50 | .55 | .60 |
| Price each, | .03 | .03 | .04 | .04 | .05 | .05 | .06 | .06 | .07 |

**Fig. 4. Brass Milled Thumb Nuts.**

| Size to fit | No. 4 | 6 | 8 | 10 | 12 | 14 |
|---|---|---|---|---|---|---|
| Threads to inch, | 32 | 32 | 32 | 24 & 32 | 23 | 20 |
| Price per Doz. | .50 | .50 | .50 | .55 | .55 | .55 |
| Price each, | .05 | .05 | .05 | .06 | .06 | .06 |

**Fig. 5. Brass Thumb Nuts, Flat.**

| Size to fit | No. 4 | 6 | 8 | 10 | 12 | 14 |
|---|---|---|---|---|---|---|
| Threads to inch, | 32 | 32 | 32 | 24 & 32 | 24 | 20 |
| Price per Doz. | .35 | .40 | .45 | .45 | .60 | .60 |
| Price each, | .04 | .04 | .05 | .05 | .06 | .06 |

**Fig. 6 & 7. Brass Thumb Nut Bolts.**

Head, 1/4 inch Square. Thread No. 6-32.

| Length, inch, | 1/2 | 3/4 | 1 |
|---|---|---|---|
| Price per Doz. | .75 | .75 | .85 |
| Price each, | .08 | .08 | .10 |

**Fig. 6 & 7. Br. Thumb Nut Bolts**

Head, 3/8 in. Square. Thread, No. 10-24

| Length, inches, | 3/4 | 1 | 1 1/4 | 1 1/2 |
|---|---|---|---|---|
| Price per Doz. | 1.10 | 1.20 | 1.30 | 1.40 |
| Price each, | .12 | .12 | .15 | .17 |

The above SCREWS ARE REGULAR MACHINE SCREW SIZES.

No. 4, 7-64. No. 6, 9-64. No. 8, 5-32. No. 10, 3-16. No. 12, 7-32. No. 14, 1-4 in.

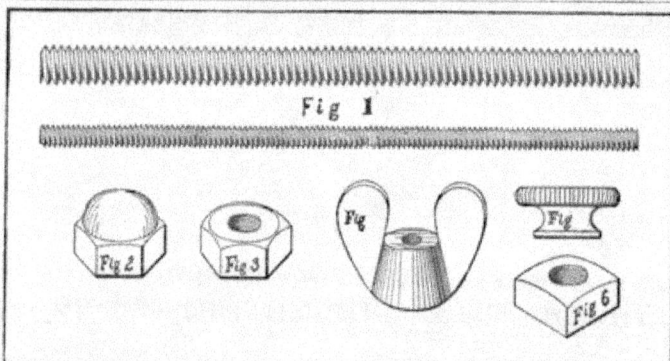

Fig 1

The above cut represents a very convenient method of making small bolts for connecting parts of models and other purposes. It consists of a piece of iron or brass rod, with a screw cut on the whole length, with nuts to fit. This rod may be cut to any desired length, and by putting a nut on each end, used as a bolt. The nut (Fig. 2) makes a very neat finish, as it is not drilled wholly through, and covers the end of the screw.

| Fig. 1. Screw Threaded Wire, | Diam. | 1/8 | 3-16 | 1/4 |
|---|---|---|---|---|
| | Threads to inch | 32 | 32 | 20 |
| | Brass, per foot | .10 | .12 | .15 |
| | Iron per foot | .08 | .10 | .12 |
| Fig. 2. Brass Cap Nuts, | Per dozen | .50 | .50 | .75 |
| " 3. Brass Hex. Nuts, | " " | .25 | .25 | .50 |
| " 6. Brass Square Nuts, | " " | .15 | .20 | .30 |
| " 6. Iron Square Nuts, | " " | .10 | .10 | .10 |
| " 5. Brass Thumb Nuts, | " " | .35 | .45 | .60 |
| " 4. Br's Milled Thumb Nuts, | " " | .50 | .50 | .50 |

Square Brass Nuts to fit Machine Screws.

| Size | 4 | 4 | 6 | 8 | 10 | 10 | 12 | 14 |
|---|---|---|---|---|---|---|---|---|
| Thread | 36 | 32 | 32 | 32 | 24 | 32 | 24 | 20 |
| Per Doz. | .15 | .15 | .15 | .17 | .20 | .20 | .25 | .30 |

# CASE OF KNURLS.

Containing 18 of the most useful patterns of Knurls,
with Holder and Screw-Driver, put up
in a neat Black Walnut Box.

PRICE, COMPLETE,     +     +     $5.00.

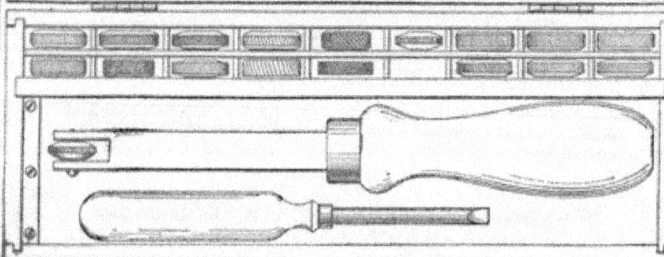

## KNURLS OR MILLING WHEELS.

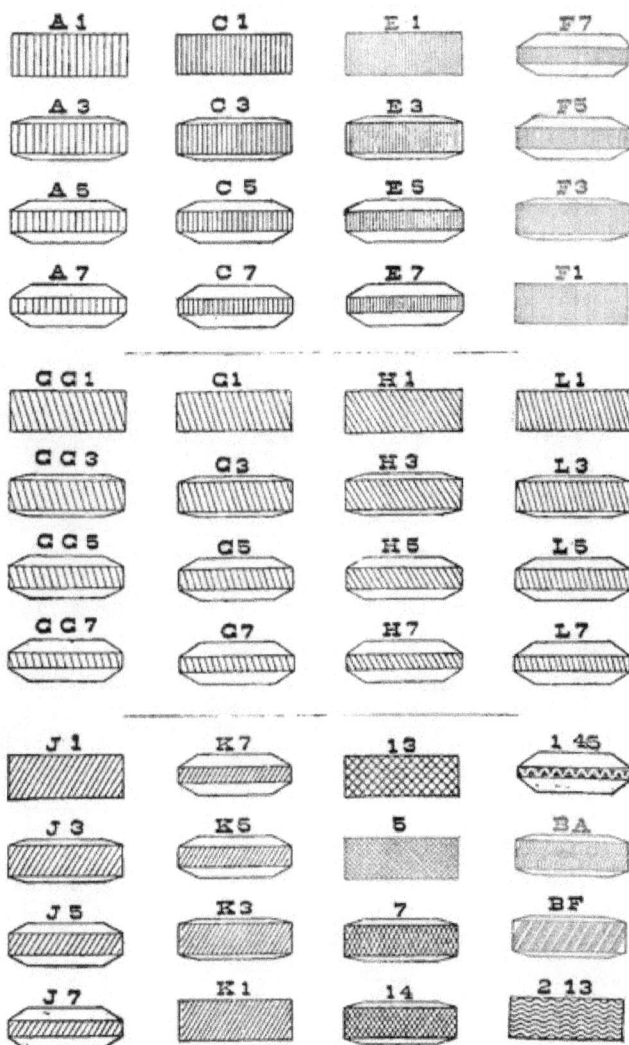

| A 1 | C 1 | E 1 | F 7 |
| C 3 | C 3 | E 3 | F 5 |
| A 5 | C 5 | E 5 | F 3 |
| A 7 | C 7 | E 7 | F 1 |

| G G 1 | G 1 | H 1 | L 1 |
| G G 3 | G 3 | H 3 | L 3 |
| G G 5 | G 5 | H 5 | L 5 |
| G G 7 | G 7 | H 7 | L 7 |

| J 1 | K 7 | 13 | 1 45 |
| J 3 | K 5 | 5 | BA |
| J 5 | K 3 | 7 | BF |
| J 7 | K 1 | 14 | 2 13 |

**PRICE OF ALL ABOVE PATTERNS 35 CTS. EACH.**

# KNURLS OR MILLING WHEELS.

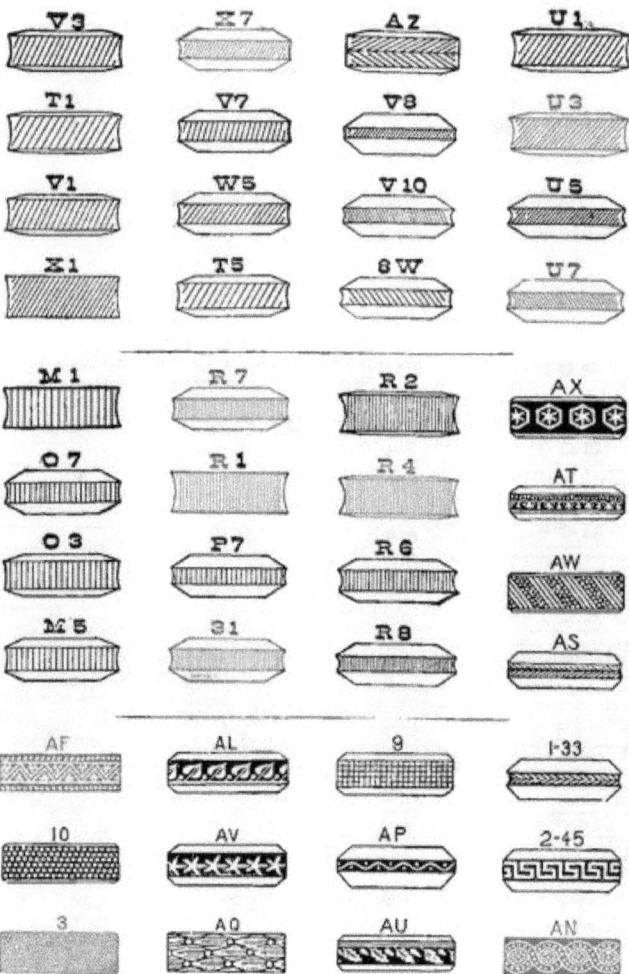

**All Cuts are exact size of KNURLS.**

PRICE OF ALL ABOVE PATTERNS 35 CTS. EACH.

# Tool Racks.

MADE OF SHEET STEEL AND NICKEL PLATED   Made in lengths
of Two Feet with Clasps of Three Sizes, viz.: 5-8 inch,
7-8 inch and 1 1-8 inch.   Price 20c. per Strip.

Suitable for hanging up Files, Tools, etc., in Factories, Workshops, Closets, Tool Chests, etc.

Nos. 230, 231 and 232.

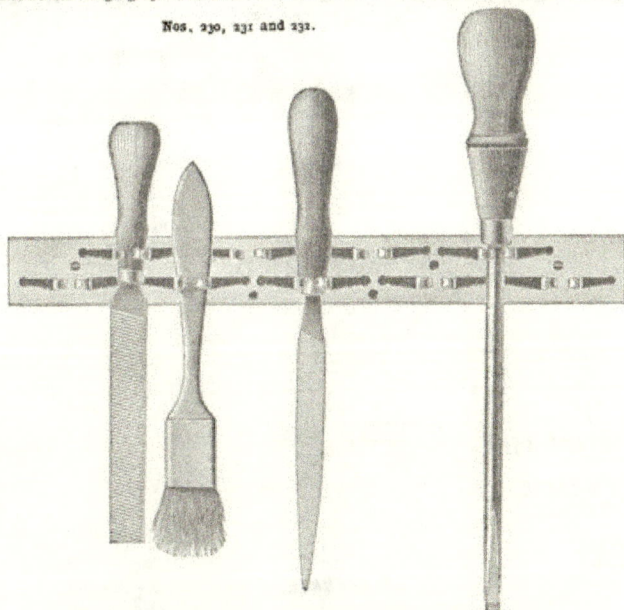

**WITH HOOKS IN PLACE OF CLASPS.   No. 240.**

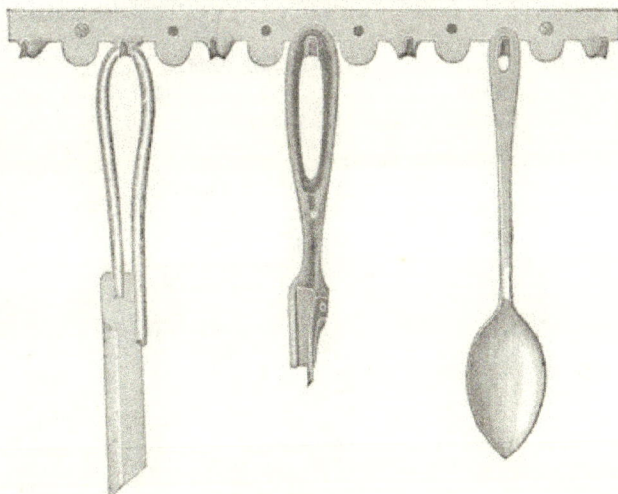

# THE CELEBRATED "MONK" MOULDERS' TOOLS.

## SQUARE TROWELS.

| Width | Length 4 in. | 4½ | 5 | 5½ | 6 Each. |
|---|---|---|---|---|---|
| 1 in. | $ .50 | $ .55 | $ .60 | $ .65 | $ .70 " |
| 1¼ " | .50 | .55 | .60 | .65 | .70 " |
| 1½ " | .60 | .65 | .70 | .75 | .80 " |
| 1¾ " | | | .80 | .85 | .90 " |
| 2 " | | | .90 | .90 | .95 " |

## HEART TROWELS.

| Width | 2 | 2¼ | 2½ | 3 inch. |
|---|---|---|---|---|
| Each | .55 | .70 | .80 | $1.05 |

## HEART AND SQUARE.

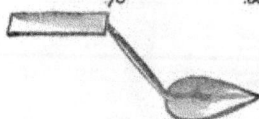

| Width | ¾ | 1 | 1¼ | 1½ | 1¾ | 2 inch. |
|---|---|---|---|---|---|---|
| Each | .45 | .50 | .60 | .70 | .80 | .85 |

## YANKEE.

| Width | ¼ | ⅝ | ¾ | 1 inch. |
|---|---|---|---|---|
| Each | .50 | .55 | .60 | .70 |

## HALF ROUND CORNER.

| Width | 1 | 1¼ | 1½ | 2 inch. |
|---|---|---|---|---|
| Each $ .60 | | | | |

## SQUARE CORNER.

| Width | 2 | 2½ | 3 inch. |
|---|---|---|---|
| Each $ .60 | | | |

## LIFTERS.

| | 10 | 12 | 14 | 16 | 18 | 20 |
|---|---|---|---|---|---|---|
| ¼ x | $ .40 | $ .45 | $ .50 | $ .55 | | |
| ⅜ x | .40 | .45 | .50 | .55 | | |
| ½ x | .45 | .50 | .55 | .60 | | |
| ⅝ x | .50 | .55 | .60 | .65 | .70 | |
| ¾ x | | .60 | .65 | .70 | .75 | |
| ⅞ x | | .65 | .70 | .75 | .80 | .85 |
| 1 x | | | .80 | .85 | .90 | .95 |
| | | | Each. | | | |

## CHANDLER & FARQUHAR, BOSTON, MASS.

### HEXAGON BRASS ROD, in Pieces 1 Ft. Long.

| | | | | | | |
|---|---|---|---|---|---|---|
| Diameter, . | 1/8 | 3/16 | 1/4 | 5/16 | 3/8 | 1/2 |
| Per Ft. . | $0.03 | .04 | .06 | .08 | .12 | .22 |

### SQUARE BRASS ROD, in Pieces 1 Ft. Long.

| | | | | | | |
|---|---|---|---|---|---|---|
| Size, . . . . | 1/8 | 3/16 | 1/4 | 5/16 | 3/8 | 1/2 |
| Per Ft. . | $0.03 | .04 | .07 | .10 | .15 | .25 |

### ROUND BRASS ROD, in Pieces 1 Ft. Long.

| | | | | | | | | | | | | | |
|---|---|---|---|---|---|---|---|---|---|---|---|---|---|
| Diameter, | 1/16 | 3/32 | 1/8 | 5/32 | 3/16 | 7/32 | 1/4 | 5/16 | 3/8 | 1/2 | 5/8 | 3/4 | 1 |
| Per Ft. | $0.02 | .02 | .03 | .03 | .04 | .05 | .06 | .08 | .12 | .16 | .25 | .30 | .65 |

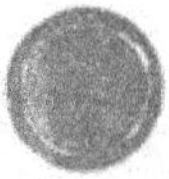

### BRASS TUBING, in Pieces 1 Ft. Long, $\frac{1}{20}$ In. Thick.

| | | | | | | | | | | | |
|---|---|---|---|---|---|---|---|---|---|---|---|
| Diameter outside, | 1/8 | 3/16 | 1/4 | 5/16 | 3/8 | 7/16 | 1/2 | 5/8 | 3/4 | 7/8 | 1 |
| Per Ft. | $0.03 | .05 | .06 | .07 | .07 | .08 | .08 | .10 | .13 | .15 | .17. |

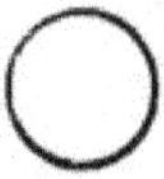

### HEXAGON BRASS TUBE, 1 Ft. Long, $\frac{1}{20}$ In. Thick.

| | | | | |
|---|---|---|---|---|
| Diameter, . | 1/4 | 5/16 | 3/8 | 1/2 |
| Per Ft. . | $0.08 | .10 | .12 | .13 |

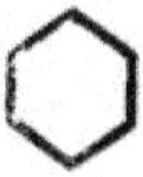

### SQUARE BRASS TUBING, 1 Ft. Long, $\frac{1}{20}$ In. Thick.

| | | | | | | |
|---|---|---|---|---|---|---|
| Diameter, . | 1/4 | 5/16 | 3/8 | 1/2 | 5/8 | 3/4 |
| Per Ft. . | $0.08 | .10 | .12 | .13 | .17 | .25 |

## SHEET BRASS.

| | | | |
|---|---|---|---|
| 1/16 in. thick, | 1/8 to 2 in. wide, | . . . . . | 5 to 20 cts. per foot. |
| 1/8 " | 1/2 to 3 " | . . . . . | 7 to 50 " " |
| 3/16 " | 1/2 to 3 " | . . . . . | 10 to 90 " " |
| 1/4 " | 1/2 to 3 " | . . . . . | 12 to $1.25 " |

## BRASS CIRCLES.

| | | | | | | | | |
|---|---|---|---|---|---|---|---|---|
| Diameter, . . . | 1 1/2 | 2 | 2 1/2 | 3 | 4 | 5 | 6 | 8 |
| Thickness, 1/16, Price each, | $0.05 | .08 | .10 | .12 | .20 | .25 | .40 | .75 |
| " 1/8 " " | .10 | .15 | .20 | .25 | .40 | .50 | .75 | 1.25 |
| " 1/4 " " | .. | .20 | .25 | .35 | .50 | .75 | 1.00 | 1.50 |

Complete Catalogue of Gears on application.

## THE ALEXANDER ADJUSTABLE JOINTER GAUGE.

We claim for this tool:

1st. The ease with which it is attached to any Plane, Jack or Jointer.

2d. The great amount of time saved, without the use of Bevel or Try-Square.

3d. Is adjustable for squaring, or to any Bevel desired.

4th. The work completed in the highest state of perfection, even by inexperienced workmen.

Attach the Gauge to the plane so that the depression in the centre of the wing of the Gauge shall be directly opposite the cutting edge of the plane iron.

Price, - $1.50 each.

# PATENT HACK SAW FRAME.

## No.3 FRAME

These Hack Saw Frames are made of Spring Steel, Japanned, and are the cheapest and best ever put on the market for the money. They are invaluable in the house for cutting a bone or nail. **Price 35 cts.**

## STEEL BENCH ANVIL.

The top is finely polished, and with the solid base, makes a very useful and attractive tool.

No. 1, length of top
3½ inches, $1.00 each.

No. 2, length of top
4 inches, $1.25 each.

## Patent Adjustable Chamfer Plane.

The front section of this Plane is movable up and down. It can be firmly secured to the rear section at any desired point by means of a thumb-screw. Without the use of any other tool, this Plane will do perfect chamfer or stop-chamfer work of all ordinary widths.

For Beading, Reeding or Moulding a chamfer, an additional section to this Plane is furnished (price $1.00) with six cutters, sharpened at both ends, including a large variety of ornamental forms.

No. 72.  Chamfer Plane, 9 inches in length, 1½ inch cutter........$1.50 net
No. 72½.  Chamfer Plane, with Beading and Moulding Attachment..2.25  "

## Stanley's Patent Bit and Square Level.

The frame of this Level has three pairs of V slots on its back edges. The shank to a Bit will lie in these slots, either parallel with the bubble-glass, at an exact angle to it, or at an angle of 45 degrees.

A Thumb-Screw secures the Level to the Bit, in either position : and boring can be done with perfect accuracy as to perpendicular, horizontal or angle of 45 degrees, by observing the bubble-glass while turning the bit.

The frame can also be attached to a Carpenter's Square. Two shoulders rest on the top of the horizontal leg to the square, thus making it an accurate Spirit-level. The upright leg of the square will indicate an exact Plumb-line.

No. 44.  Bit and Square Level, Brass Frame, in a box, each.......$0.30 net

## Stanley's Improved Level Sights.

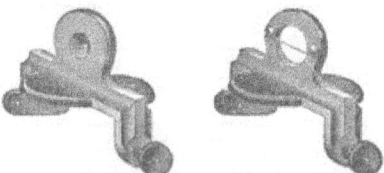

By the use of these ingenious devices, which can be attached to any Level, the owner has a convenient and accurate means for leveling, from one given point to another at a long distance away. When not in use the Level Sights are easily detached, and can be packed away in a small space for future use.

No. 1.  Improved Level Sights, per pair in a box................$0.75 net

# J. R. Duff's Drilling Attachment.

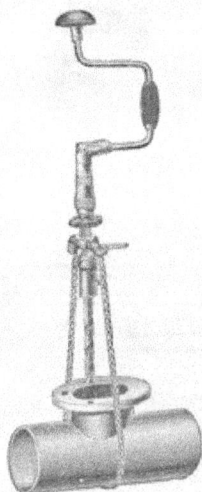 

Style A.                    Style B.

This is the best hand drill ever invented for its class of work, it has a bearing of steel balls which reduces the friction to the minimum. Every thickness of steel, iron or metal of any kind can easily be drilled with any sized drill up to and including one inch.

It can be operated with any ordinary bit brace, and requires no skill by the operator. It saves time and labor. Every mechanic should have one. Style A has one screw chuck and will hold round shanked drills only. Style B has a universal chuck and is best adapted to holding square shanked drills.

All orders by mail will receive prompt attention.

| | | | | |
|---|---|---|---|---|
| STYLE A EACH, | - | - | - | $1.50 |
| STYLE B " | - | - | - | 2.00 |

We keep in stock a complete line of

## STARRETT'S FINE MECHANI-CAL TOOLS,

Consisting of CALIPERS, DIVIDERS, STEEL RULES, SQUARES, &c.,

And a catalogue will be sent on application to us.

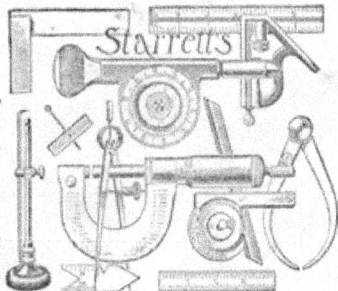

## Linemen's Climbers.

| | | |
|---|---|---|
| Per pair, without Straps. | Dicks' | $2.00 |
| " " " | Weldon's | 2.50 |
| Straps per set of four | | 1.00 |

## Splicing Clamps.

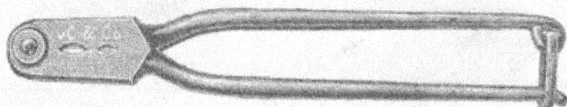

Each .................................................................. $1.25

## Lineman's Vise.

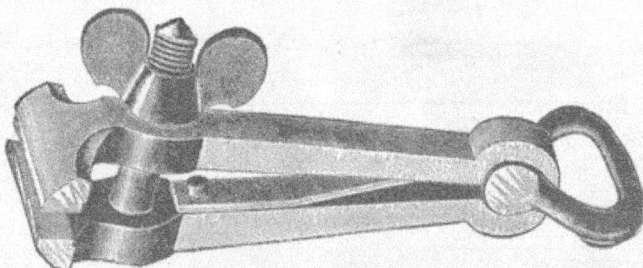

| | |
|---|---|
| Stub's (English) Looped, 5½ inch | $3.50 |
| Extra quality (German) Looped, 5½ inch | 2.50 |
| Strap extra | 1.00 |

## Telephone Wire Snips.

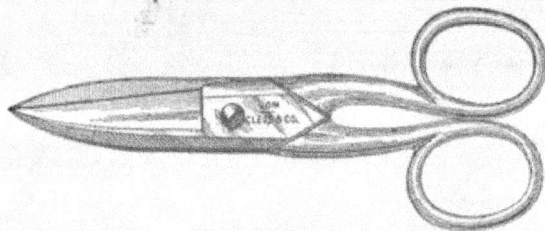

Extra Quality Cast Steel. Nickel Plated, 5½ inch, each ................ $1.00

## Disston Hand Saws.

| Length of Blade, inch, | 16 | 18 | 20 | 22 | 24 | 26 |
|---|---|---|---|---|---|---|
| Price, each, | $1.00 | 1.08 | 1.22 | 1.35 | 1.45 | 1.53 |

### Back Saws.

| Length of Blade, inch, | 8 | 10 | 12 | 14 | 16 |
|---|---|---|---|---|---|
| Price, each, | $1.00 | 1.08 | 1.20 | 1.35 | 1.53 |

### Compass Saws.

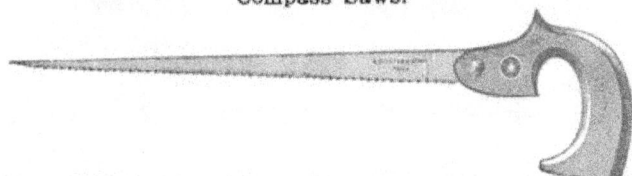

| Length of Blade, inch, | 10 | 12 | 14 | 16 |
|---|---|---|---|---|
| Price, each, | $ .35 | .38 | .42 | .50 |

### Try Square.
#### With graduated steel blade.

| Inch, | 4½ | 6 | 7½ | 9 | 12 |
|---|---|---|---|---|---|
| Each, | $ .25 | .30 | .35 | .40 | .50 |

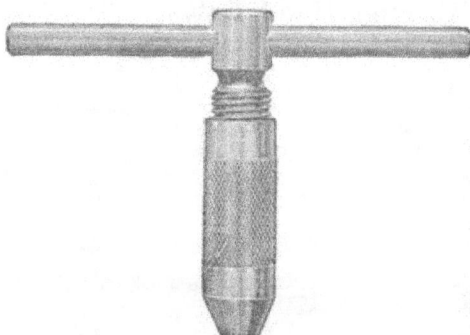
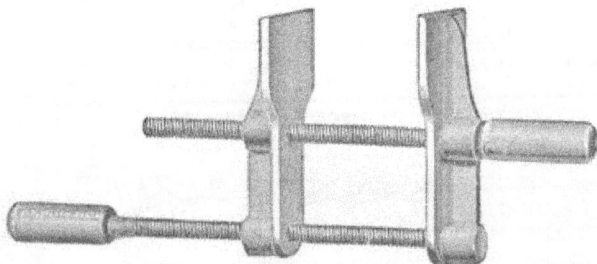

CHANDLER & FARQUHAR, BOSTON, MASS.

## BURNER PLYERS.

(POLISHED.)

| | | | |
|---|---|---|---|
| Size, | 5 | 6 | 7 |
| Price, each, | $0.50 | .55 | .60 |

## PEASE COMBINATION PLYERS.

Gas Plyers, Wire Cutters, Wrench and Screw Driver combined. Drop forged from best tool steel, and finished first-class; a very convenient tool for all mechanics, and very handy in every house. By shifting from one hole to the other it changes from size of gas burner to ½ inch pipe, or from $\frac{3}{16}$ inch to 1 inch round.

Price, Nickel plated, $1.25 each.

### Something New.

## Hall's Improved Pipe Wrench.

It will cost less for repairs than any other Pipe Wrench.

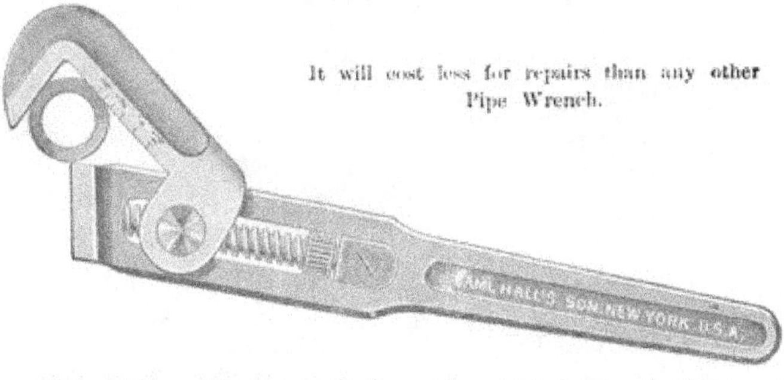

Grips quickly and firmly *galvanized* as well as other pipe, *and will not crush it.* Releases instantly. *Cannot lock on the pipe.* Has scale to set the wrench to size before placing on pipe. Can be sharpened on grindstone or emery wheel without taking apart. Jaws are smooth and will not mar a nut or polished fitting. It has other attractive features.

| | | | | | |
|---|---|---|---|---|---|
| Length Open, | 6 | 10 | 14 | 18 | 24 |
| Size of Pipe, | ⅛ to ½ | ⅛ to ¾ | ¼ to 1¼ | ¼ to 1½ | ½ to 2½ |
| Largest Opening for Nut or Bolt, | ¾ | $1\frac{5}{16}$ | 1¾ | 2¼ | 3¼ |
| Price, each. | $1.00 | 1.25 | 1.50 | 2.00 | 3.00 |

## FLAT-NOSE PLYERS.

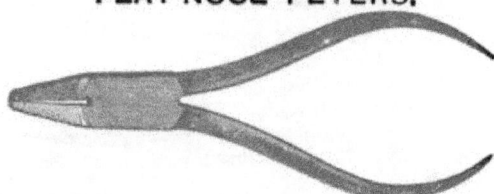

| Size, Inches, | | | | 3 | 3½ | 4 | 4½ | 5 | 6 | 7 | 8 |
|---|---|---|---|---|---|---|---|---|---|---|---|
| P. S. Stubs', | | | | $0.50 | .50 | .50 | .50 | .55 | .80 | 1.25 | 1.75 |
| German, | | | | .30 | .30 | .30 | .30 | .35 | .40 | .60 | .80 |

Malleable Iron Flat Plyers, to 4½ inches, 15 cts. per pair.

## END-CUTTING NIPPERS.

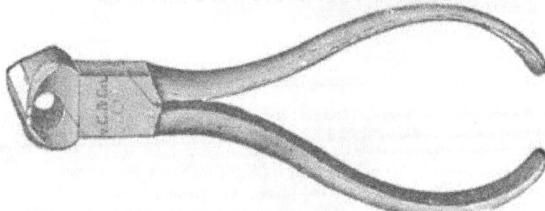

| Size, inches, | | | | to 4 | 4½ | 5 | 5½ | 6 | 7 | 8 |
|---|---|---|---|---|---|---|---|---|---|---|
| P. S. Stubs', | | | | $0.90 | .90 | .90 | 1.00 | 1.25 | 1.70 | 2.10 |
| German, | | | | .60 | .60 | .60 | .70 | .75 | 1.00 | 1.25 |

## BELL-HANGERS' OR SIDE-CUTTING PLYERS.

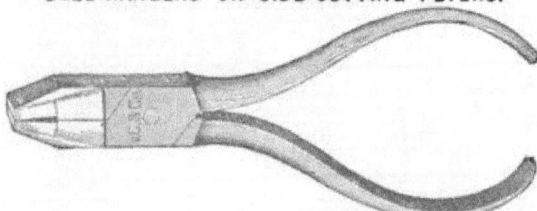

| Size, inches, | | | | 4 | 4½ | 5 | 5½ | 6 | 7 | 8 |
|---|---|---|---|---|---|---|---|---|---|---|
| P. S Stubs', | | | | $0.90 | .90 | .90 | .90 | 1.00 | 1.50 | 2.00 |
| German, | | | | .65 | .65 | .65 | .. | .80 | 1.00 | 1.15 |

Also, in stock, Long Flat-Nose Plyers; and Stockinger or Reed Plyers, with smooth jaws.

## ROUND-NOSE PLYERS.

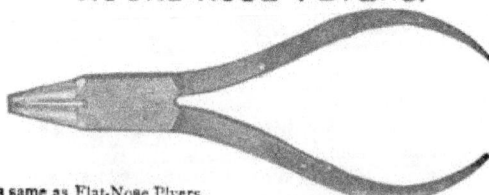

**Prices** same as Flat-Nose Plyers.

# What Now?

Well, well, well, how awfully off is that fellow who tries to get a first-class Engineer to buy, or even to try "Something just as good."

There is only one BEST Metal Polish.

*YOU want it,*
    *WE'VE got it,*
        *PRESTOLINE is its name.*

### SHALL WE SEND YOU A SAMPLE?

It cleans as it is rubbed on and polishes as it is wiped off.

| Sizes, | Trial, | ½ pt. | Quart. | ½ gal. | Gal. |
|--------|--------|-------|--------|--------|------|
| Prices, | $ .10 | .25 | .75 | 1.25 | 2.40 |

# KEENAN'S PROTRACTOR.

A glance at this cut will, no doubt, convince you of its usefulness. The PROTRACTOR is made of sheet steel, 1-16 of an inch thick and 2 inches square, is highly finished, and can be attached to any bevel gauge, by means of an eccentric lever, which can be adjusted to any size. On one side of the Protractor is a thread and centre gauge, which, with the Protractor, makes three tools in one. The circular edge or arc is accurately graduated. By placing the Protractor on the bevel gauge, and moving the indicator to the required degrees, it is set in an instant. One of the advantages of this tool is, that it costs but a trifle compared with a bevel protractor, and can be used as a thread and centre gauge and protractor combined, where a bevel protractor can only be used as a protractor. Another advantage is, that when not in use it can be removed from the bevel-gauge in a moment.

**Protractor (without bevel),** - - - - - - - - **$1.00**

# "PARAGON" SPEED INDICATOR.

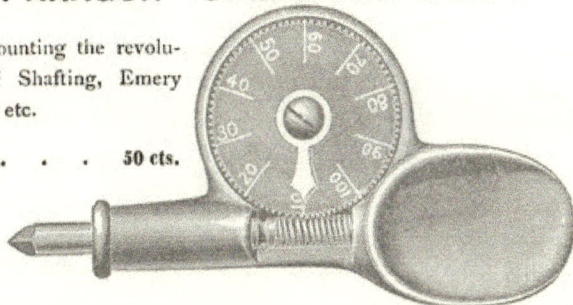

For counting the revolutions of Shafting, Emery Wheels, etc.

**PRICE,** - - - **50 cts.**

# The Bernard Patent Pliers.

## Open Throat Parallel Jaws.

Are constructed on a new principle, being made of **Crucible Steel** throughout, and **Full Nickel Plated.**

The Cutting Pliers have **Interchangeable Parts**, which can easily and cheaply be replaced, when worn, or broken.

It is acknowledged by all who use them, that their **Durability** and **Gripping, or Cutting Power** is double that of any other Plier in the market.

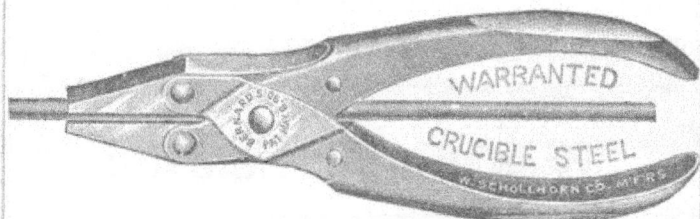

Flat Nose Plier— { Size, 4½ 5½ 6½ 7½ (extra heavy) inch.
{ Price, each, $ .50 .65 .85 1.10

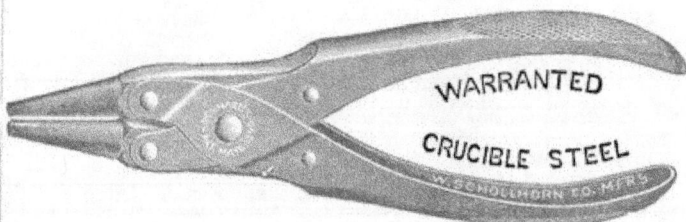

Round Nose Plier— { Size, 4½ 5½ 6½ inch.
{ Price, each, $ .50 .65 .85

Cutting Plier— { Size, 4½ 5½ 6½ 7½ (extra heavy) inch.
{ Price, $ .80 1.05 1.25 1.65

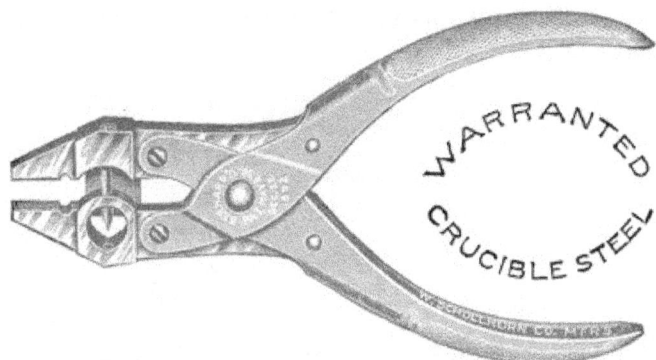

Sewing Machine Plier—Price, $1.00 each.

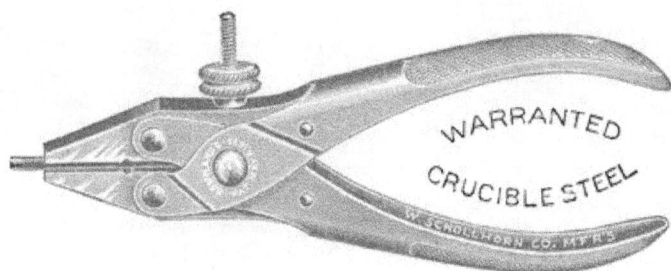

Bernard's Patent Vise Plier—Size, 6¼ inch.   Price, $1.00.

This is a Parallel Plier and Hand Vise combined and is always ready to use either as a Plier, Hand Vise, Clamp or Wrench. When used as a wrench for small bolts, nuts, set screws, &c., is superior to a screw or monkey wrench.

The surprising merits of this Plier are soon recognized by all when in use and universally pronounced the most convenient and handy tool in a workshop, factory, or wherever used by all who have used them.

## Eureka   Polishing
## Head.

This head has a steel spindle, a flange for holding circular saws or wheels, and a chuck for holding drills, it is handsomely japanned and ornamented, and presents a very neat and attractive appearance.

Price, $1.25 each.

# CARPENTERS'
# BENCH VISE.

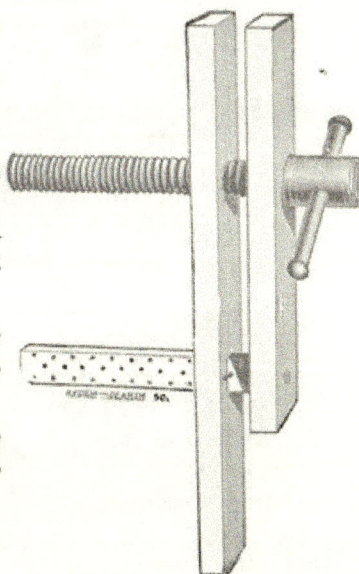

Carpenters' Vise with 2⅜ in. Hickory Screw, 36 in. high,  **$2.50.**

Carpenters' Vise with 2 in. Hickory Screw, 36 in. high,  **$2.00.**

Amateurs' Vise with 1¾ in. Hickory Screw,  **$1.50.**

# Olmsted's Improved Mitre Boxes.

The frame is made of hard wood of the best quality selected for the purpose, and made from boards one-inch thick, and consists of two upright pieces, which are fastened rigidly to the edges of a bottom board. Has adjustable iron saw guides for any thickness of saw blade. The saw cannot cut the frame away. An ordinary cross-cut saw can be used as well as a back saw. When putting the saw into the slots in the Mitre Box have the teeth of the saw below the iron saw guides. The iron work is painted and varnished and the frames are finished in hard oil varnish, making them impervious to the action of the atmosphere.

Upon the upper edge and at one end of the uprights are fastened two irons which are used to guide the saw when sawing a square cut.

Price,  No. 1 will take work 1½ in. x 3 in.  .  .  .  .  .  $1.00
Price,  No. 2 will take work 2½ in. x 4 in.  .  .  .  .  .  1.50

## MACHINISTS' CHESTS.

Made of selected Chestnut, trimmed with Black Walnut mouldings. Black Walnut Panels, and nicely finished.

No. 28, with 2 Drawers, . . . . . . . . . . $4.50
Receptacle under Cover 18 x 10 x 2½. Sliding Tray under Cover, 16¾ x 5½ x 1¾.
First Drawer, 17 x 8¾ x 1½. Second Drawer, 17 x 8¾ x 2½.

No. 29, with 3 Drawers, . . . . . . . . . . $6.00
Receptacle under Cover, 21 x 11½ x 3½. Sliding Tray under Cover, 20 x 6 5-16 x 1½.
First Drawer, 20 x 10 9-16 x 1. Second Drawer, 20 x 10 9-16 x 1¾.
Third Drawer, 20 x 10 9-16 x 2½.

## Malleable Iron Chains.

**With Detachable Links, and Cast-Iron Wheels with Cast Teeth.**

We can furnish any size of this chain from No. 25, 13.3 links to foot, having 75 pounds' working strain, to No. 160, links one foot in length, having 4,000 pounds' working strain. We can also furnish wheels to fit.

The wheels furnished usualy have the teeth cast. We can furnish to order, at extra cost, wheels with cut teeth. The latter should be ordered for high speed.

**Chain No. 25.**

13.3 links to the foot.

Working strain, 75 pounds.

Approximate in leather belt, one single belt.

Full size. Price per ft., 12 cts.

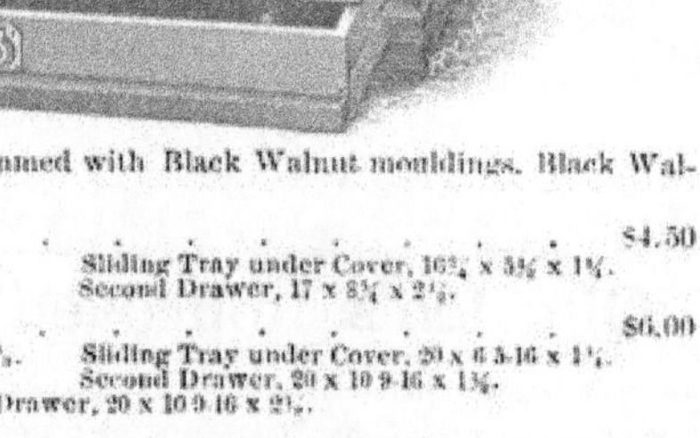

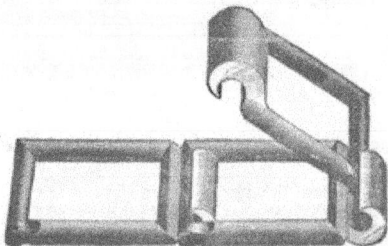

# BROWN & SHARPE STANDARD STEEL RULES.

| Length, in. . . . | 1 | 2 | 3 | 4 | 6 | 9 | 12 | 18 | 24 | 36 |
|---|---|---|---|---|---|---|---|---|---|---|
| Price each . . . | $0.15 | .25 | .35 | .45 | .65 | 1.00 | 1.25 | 2.00 | 2.75 | 7.00 |

# WRENCHES.
## GENUINE COE'S PATENT.

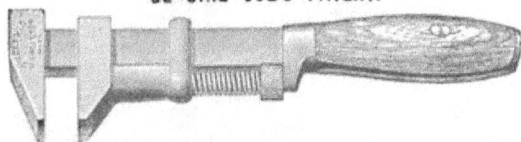

| Size, inches . . . | 4 | 6 | 8 | 10 | 12 | 15 | 18 | 21 |
|---|---|---|---|---|---|---|---|---|
| Price each, Bright . | $0.50 | .55 | .60 | .75 | .85 | 1.35 | 1.60 | 1.90 |
| "   "   Black . | | .50 | .55 | .65 | .75 | 1.25 | 1.50 | 1.80 |

## BAXTER'S PATENT "S" OR DIAGONAL.

| Size, inches . . | | 4 | 6 | 8 | 10 | 12 |
|---|---|---|---|---|---|---|
| Price, each. . . | | $0.40 | .55 | .75 | 1.15 | 1.50 |

## BRIGGS' PIPE WRENCH.

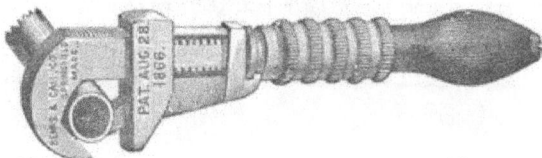

| Size, inches . . . . . . | 10 | 12 | 15 |
|---|---|---|---|
| Price each . . . . . . . . . | $1.60 | 1.80 | 2.50 |

## STILLSON'S PATENT CYLINDER WRENCH.

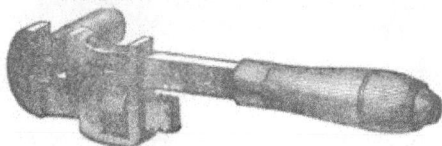

| Size, inches . . . . | 6 | 8 | 10 | 14 | 18 |
|---|---|---|---|---|---|
| Takes pipe, inch. . . | ⅛ to ½ | ⅛ to ¾ | ⅛ to 1 | ¼ to 1½ | ¾ to 2 |
| Price each. . . . . | $1.00 | 1.00 | 1.13 | 1.50 | 2.00 |

# CARVING TOOLS.

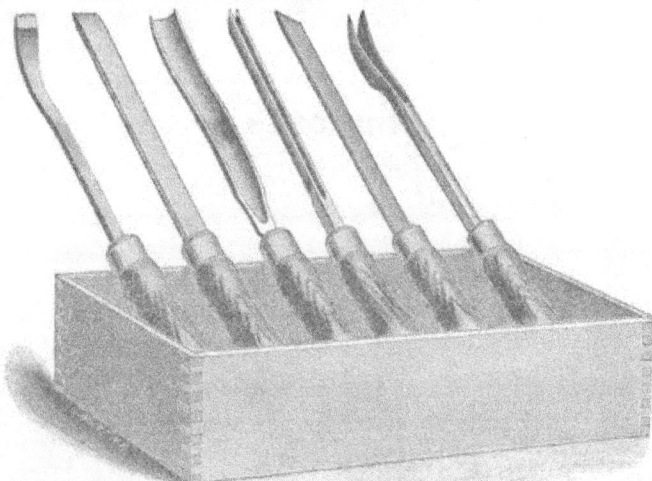

Six Tools in a Wooden Box.        Price, per set.  $1.00

These Tools are forged from best quality of steel. and are fully warranted. They have Rose-wood Handles and are sharpened ready for use.

## No. 2. Bracket Sets.

These sets are packed in paper boxes, and embrace a Spring Steel Saw Frame, polished and nickel-plated, 5 x 12 inches, having patent Clamps for holding the Saw Blades. rose-wood handle.

Fifty full-sized designs, embracing a great variety of fancy and useful articles: six Saw Blades, one awl, one Sheet of Impression Paper, and full directions for using the Saw.

Price,     .                                   $1.25

A large assortment of Chucks, Drills, Screw Plates, Files, etc., constantly in stock.

# NEW ROGERS SAW.

This season we have added all the improvements that our ingenuity can suggest, and have no hesitancy in declaring our

## NEW ROGERS SAW

to be the best low-priced saw offered to the public.

The entire frame-work is made from iron, painted and japanned black, ornamented with red and gilt stripes.

The arbors are made of steel and are carefully gauged and fitted to their bearings.

The Arms and Pitman are of the best selected ash.

All parts made to interchange, and our Jig Saw possesses **every improvement and advantage claimed** for any other in the market.

Each machine is set up and carefully inspected before leaving our works. It is then taken down and packed in a box.

While the New Rogers Saw is very rich, though not gaudy in appearance, it has been our object more especially to make, for the least possible money, a saw characterized for its Compactness, Strength and Durability, ease of action and firmness when in operation.

With each machine we give 12 Saw Blades, Wrench, Sheet of Designs, and Three Drill Points.  Price, $3.50

Orders solicited for model work, special taps or dies, etc.

# WIRE STRAIGHTENER.

This Straightener is of an improved pattern and will straighten wire from No. 3 to No. 20.

Price, . . . . . . . . . . . . . . . $12.00

# Foot Power Emery Grinder.

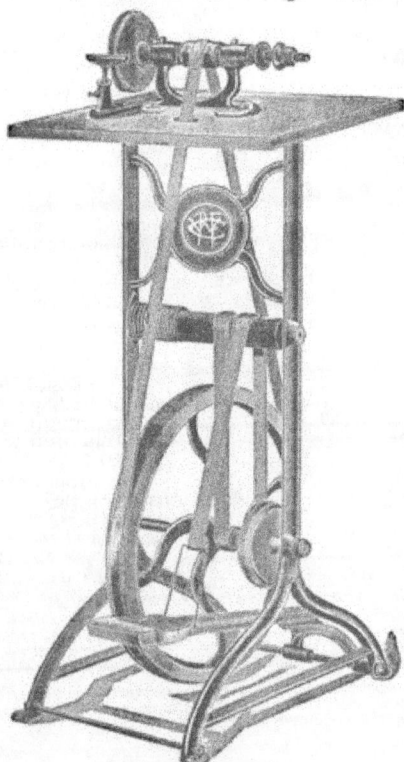

## DESCRIPTION.

Size on floor, 16x24 inches; height of table, 38 inches, size of table, 15x22 inches. A heavy fly wheel, 19 inches in diameter for 1¼ inch belt; frame of cast iron, well braced. Weight of machine, complete, 130 lbs. Head spindle ¾ inch steel, 12 inches long; has two inch collar at both ends, is fitted for wheel with ⅝ inch hole. Has a two inch turned pulley; spindle runs in 2 inch adjustable boxes; oil holes have caps to keep out dust. The head will carry two wheels 7 inches in diameter and one inch thick, or less, and 4 inches from centre of spindle to the table. The iron work is neatly painted, and is well finished throughout.

The machine is driven by Chapman's Positive Action Clutch, in which there is practically no lost motion, and is the strongest driving foot-power ever placed upon the market. They will grind three times as fast and do much nicer work than a grindstone. They are a practical tool for Carpenters, Cabinetmakers, Blacksmiths, Gunsmiths, Wagonmakers, Stonecutters, and many others, who will find they can save files and save time by using this machine, not only for grinding tools, but for much other work for which files are commonly used. A speed of 3000 per minute can be easily attained. It is a thoroughly practical polishing lathe for Nickel Platers, Jewelers and Dentists, and a polishing head will be furnished to order, if desired. **Price $15.00.**

## Olmstead's Improved Mitre Box.

The frame is made of the best quality of hard wood selected for the purpose from boards one inch thick, and consists of two upright pieces which are fastened rigidly to the edges of a bottom board. Has adjustable iron saw guides for any thickness of saw blades, the saw cannot out the frame away.

An ordinary cutting-off saw can be used as well as a back saw.

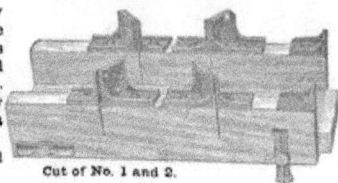

Cut of No. 1 and 2.

| Nos. | 1 | 2 | 3 | 4 |
|---|---|---|---|---|
| Takes work, | 1½ x 3 | 2½ x 4 | 1½ x 3 | 2½ x 4 |
| Price, each, | $1.00 | $1.50 | $1.25 | $1.75 |

## Forest City Screwdriver.

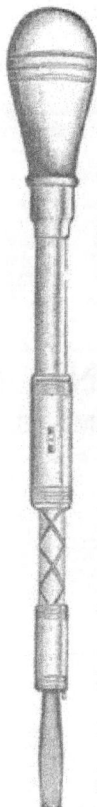

This tool contains many changes, such as a driver to push a screw in, a driver to push a screw out, a driver which will make an automatic drill, a driver that will make a continuous drill, a driver which will ratchet a screw in and out, a driver that is a ratchet wherever you catch the spindle, a driver that is stationary at long and short range. In other words, we give you a driver with different combinations; that were you to purchase the same separately would cost you a ten dollar note, and we sell you this tool with all of the above for the low price of a dollar and a half.

This driver is warranted to do all we claim for it if properly handled. We don't put it upon the market as a hammer or chisel. In order that one may become an expert in handling this driver please read carefully the following instructions:

1st. To push a screw in always have both shippers next to handle.

2nd. To push a screw out push plain shipper towards the blade.

3rd. To make continuous drill push marked shipper towards the blade, plain shipper towards the handle.

4th. To make automatic drill keep both shippers towards the blade.

5th. To make stationary driver at short range push both shippers towards the blade.

6th. To make stationary driver at long range push both shippers towards handle.

7th. To make ratchet driver to ratchet a screw in push marked shipper towards the blade, plain shipper towards the handle.

8th. To ratchet a screw out push marked shipper towards handle, plain shipper towards the blade.

9th. In attempting to remove a screw which starts hard always use the ratchet to start same and then use the push; also in pushing in a screw push until you hang up and then ratchet in. After one handles the tool a few times and gets the different combinations he soon becomes an expert and saves many hours of time, and has a tool that no money will buy.

10th. To remove the blade just slip the thumb easily down over the spring, pulling on blade at same time. Same motion in removing a drill.

## IMPROVED NICKEL-PLATED FLOOR PUSH.

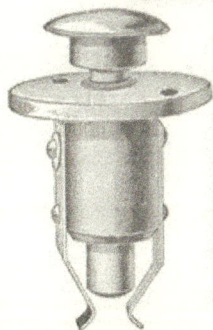

This is the most desirable foot-push made. The push is removable and has a shoulder to prevent the insulated body being pushed out in case it is stepped on. There is a hole clear through the body of the push, thus providing an escape for dust.

(Cut full size.)

No. 1. Floor Push.    Price, 50 cents.

## ELECTRIC DOOR BELL PULLS.

No. 3. A, Light Bronze; B, Dark Bronze; X, Inlaid.

No. 3 is a figured Bronze Pull, Light or Inlaid.    Price, $1.50.

## DOOR BELL-PULL ATTACHMENTS.

Designed for connecting a mechanical door pull to ring an electric bell. It can be attached without displacing the bell-pull already in use, and may be arranged to operate both the mechanical and electric bells.    Price, 30 cents.

## IMPROVED BURGLAR ALARM DOOR SPRING.

The most serviceable spring made and the easiest to put in. Large quantities are being sold.

Price, 25 cents.

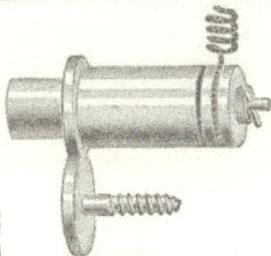

## BINDING POSTS, CONNECTORS, ETC.

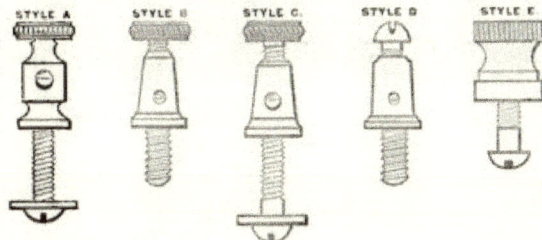

STYLE A    STYLE B    STYLE C    STYLE D    STYLE E

### PRICE LIST.

| Style. | Each. |
|---|---|
| A | .10 |
| B | .10 |
| C | .10 |
| D | .08 |
| E | .10 |

Samson Battery,
each, $1.10

Push Button,
each, .10

Electric Bell,
each, .75

Insulated Wire,
per lb. .30

Electrician Staples,
per lb. .20

## Screw-Drivers.

### NOVELTY.

This figure shows the screw driver with the blade projected for use. It is entirely self-operating and only requires the use of one hand to instantaneously project or retract the blade. Price, 50 cents.

## Magazine Screw-Driver.

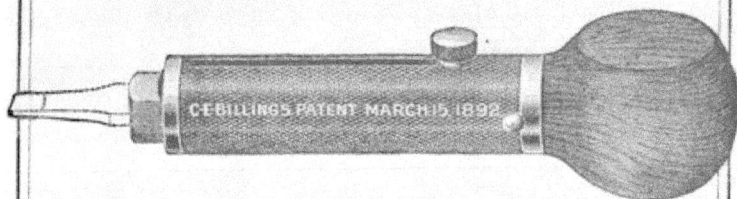

This is a neat, compact tool, containing four sizes of screw drivers within the handle, the blades are pivoted to the slide, and by raising the locking bolt and pressing forward the slide the blades will swing out. Select the size wanted, draw the slide back into the handle, and the driver is ready for use. Whole length when closed is 3¼ inches. Price, each, $1.00

## Cast-steel Wing Calipers.  Cast-steel Wing Dividers.

| Size,in. | 5 | 6 | 7 | 8 | 10 | 12 | 15 |
|---|---|---|---|---|---|---|---|
| Price, | .40 | .45 | .50 | .60 | .65 | .90 | 1.25 |

| Size,in. | 5 | 6 | 8 | 10 | 12 | 15 | 18 |
|---|---|---|---|---|---|---|---|
| Price, | .50 | .60 | .75 | .92 | 1.10 | 1.60 | 2.25 |

## Call's Patent Inside Calipers.

| Size . . . . | 4 | 6 |
|---|---|---|
| Price each . . | $0.75 | .85 |

## REGISTER CALIPERS.

3-inch.  3-inch.

Nickel-plated.  Measuring inside or out.

| 3-inch, price each | . . . . . . . . . . . | $0.60 |
|---|---|---|
| 5   "   "   " | . . . . . . . . . . . | .90 |
| 6   "   "   " | . . . . . . . . . . . | 1.00 |

## Cast-steel Navy Calipers.

5-inch.

3½ inch, price each . . . . . . . . . . $0.40

## Double Calipers.

| Size, in. . . . | 2½ | 4 | 6 |
|---|---|---|---|
| Price each . . | $0.35 | .40 | .50 |

# New Little Giant Screw Plates.

(A complete catalogue of these on application.)

| No. a 1. | Cuts $\frac{1}{8}$ to $\frac{1}{4}$— 5 sizes. | Price, | $ 6.50 |
|---|---|---|---|
| " a 2. | " $\frac{1}{8}$ to $\frac{1}{4}$— 7 " | " | 8.00 |
| " a 3. | " $\frac{5}{64}$ to $\frac{1}{4}$—10 " | " | 10.50 |
| 1. | " $\frac{1}{4}$ to $\frac{1}{2}$— 5 " | " | 12.00 |
| 2. | " $\frac{1}{4}$ to $\frac{5}{8}$— 5 " | " | 13.50 |
| 3. | " $\frac{5}{8}$ to 1 — 4 " | " | 15.00 |
| 4. | " $\frac{1}{2}$ to 1 — 5 " | " | 17.50 |
| 5. | " $\frac{1}{4}$ to $\frac{5}{8}$— 7 " | " | 16.00 |
| 6. | " $\frac{3}{8}$ to 1 — 7 " | " | 22.00 |

# The Lightning Screw Plate.

The screws cut with it are far more perfect than can be made with ordinary dies, and equal to the best lathe work, being neatly and sharply cut in the bolts instead of being jammed out of the iron. No burr is raised above the true size.

| No. O. | Cuts $\frac{1}{8}$ to $\frac{1}{4}$—5 sizes. | Price, | $ 5.50 |
|---|---|---|---|
| O. | " $\frac{1}{8}$ to $\frac{1}{4}$—7 " | " | 7.00 |
| A. | " $\frac{3}{16}$ to $\frac{5}{16}$—5 " | " | 8.00 |
| B. | " $\frac{1}{4}$ to $\frac{5}{8}$—7 " | " | 16.00 |
| C. | " $\frac{1}{2}$ to 1 —5 " | " | 18.50 |
| L. | " $\frac{1}{4}$ to 1 —9 " | " | 27.50 |

(A more complete catalogue on application.)

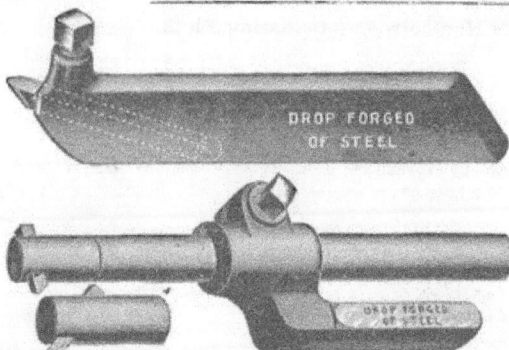

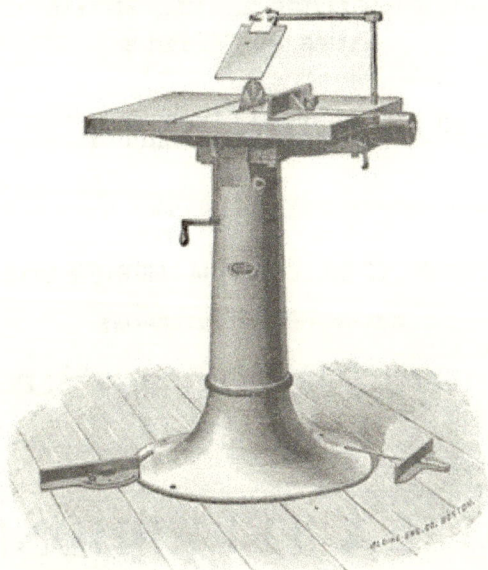

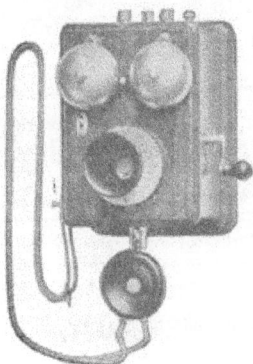

## Parker's Patent Parallel Victor Vises.

These Vises have self-adjusting back jaws, which automatically adapt themselves for holding wedge shaped pieces.

| No. | | | | | PLAIN BASE. Weight. | each. | SWIVEL BASE. Weight. | each. |
|---|---|---|---|---|---|---|---|---|
| 370 | Length of Jaws, | 3½ | in. | | 25 lbs. | $ 6.50 | 30 lbs. | $ 7.00 |
| 371 | " | " | 3½ | " | 39 " | 7.00 | 42 " | 8.50 |
| 372 | " | " | 4½ | " | 57 " | 10.00 | 60 " | 12.50 |
| 373 | " | " | 5 | " | 73 " | 14.00 | 78 " | 16.00 |
| 374 | " | " | 5½ | " | 98 " | 17.00 | 110 " | 19.00 |
| 375 | " | " | 6¼ | " | 150 " | 24.00 | 165 " | 27.00 |

The Steel Faces of these Vises are Milled and fitted to the Jaws, and are renewable at a trifling cost.

## LEWIS' PATENT DOUBLE STEEL SLIDE BAR VISES.

| No. | Width Jaw | Opens. | PLAIN BASE. Weight. | Each. | SWIVEL BASE. Weight. | Each. |
|---|---|---|---|---|---|---|
| 3 | 2¼ in. | 3½ in. | 18 lbs. | $ 5.50 | 22 lbs. | $ 6.75 |
| 5 | 3 " | 4 " | 25 " | 6.25 | 29 " | 7.50 |
| 7 | 3½ " | 5 " | 33 " | 7.00 | 38 " | 8.50 |
| 9 | 4 " | 6 " | 54 " | 9.00 | 60 " | 10.50 |
| 11 | 4½ " | 7 " | 70 " | 10.50 | 78 " | 12.50 |
| 13 | 5 " | 8 " | 105 " | 16.00 | 120 " | 18.00 |
| 15 | 5½ " | 9 " | 125 " | 18.00 | 142 " | 21.00 |
| 17 | 6½ " | 10 " | 165 " | 24.00 | 185 " | 27.00 |
| 19 | 7½ " | 12 " | 198 " | 30.00 | 225 " | 35.00 |

Complete catalogues of above vises on application.

## The Eclipse Scraper.

In introducing this tool to the carpenters and woodworkers generally, we feel we are supplying a long felt want for a handy and efficient scraper; one that can be used in almost every place where one would have occasion to use such a tool. It is very effective on hard wood floors, as it will do more and better work, and much easier, than any other scraper on the market.

Price, $1.50.

[Patent Applied For.]

## The Brighton Hand Vise.

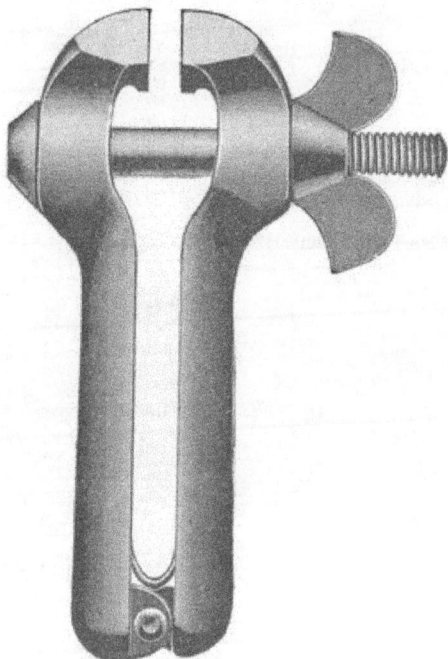

This Vise is a casting nicely japanned, with a heavy spring inside to open the jaws, which are closed with a bolt and nut, as seen in the cut. It has a blue finish on the jaws.

| | | | |
|---|---|---|---|
| Length, | 4 in. | 4¼ in. | 4¾ in. |
| Width of jaw, | 1 in. | 1¼ in. | 1⅜ in. |
| Price, each, | $ .20 | .25 | 30 |

# The "Boss" Hand Vise.

The jaws are 1¼ inch wide, length of tool over all 6 inch, and opens ¾ inch—weighs 8 oz.

The jaws opening parallel it will grip firmer than the old style of vise, it is strong and well made, and at its extremely low price for so good an article, it has had a large sale.

This vise is all steel hardened throughout and finely finished with polished jaws.

Price, 60 Cents.

# Carew's Patent Wire Cutter.

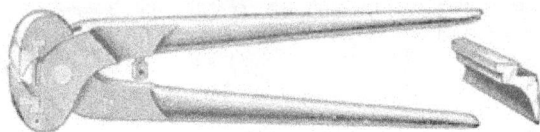

**MADE THROUGHOUT OF FORGED STEEL.**

The adjustable jaws are the main feature, these are made of the best tool steel and are brought to a cutting edge before being tempered. The cutting quality is unsurpassed.

Whenever they become dulled by use, they can be removed readily by driving from the end showing prick marks, and replaced after ground, thus obviating the necessity of buying new cutters.

| Length. | 6 in. | 8 in. | 10 in. | 12 in. | 14 in. |
|---|---|---|---|---|---|
| Price, | $1.75 | $2.00 | $2.25 | $2.60 | $3.00 |
| Extra Jaws, | .50 | .55 | .60 | .65 | .70 |

# MATHEMATICAL INSTRUMENTS.

## INSTRUMENTS IN CASES.

**No. 3.**—Mahogany Case, containing 7 pieces, BRASS, 1 pair Compasses, 4¼ inch, with Pen, Pencil Points, and Lengthening Bar; 1 Crayon Holder; 1 Protractor; 1 Rule. Price, each, . . . . . . $0 75

**No. 4.**—Mahogany Case, containing 8 pieces, BRASS, 1 pair Compasses, 4¼ inch, with Pen, Pencil Points, and Lengthening Bar; 1 Drawing Pen; 1 Protractor; 1 Crayon Holder; 1 Rule. Price, each, . . 1 00

**No. 18.**—Same as No. 4, but with 5½ inch Compasses and 4¼ inch Dividers. Price, each, . . . . . . . . . . . . . . 1 35

**No. 47.**—Mahogany Case, containing 12 pieces, BRASS, 1 pair Compasses, 4½ inch, with Pen, Pencil Points, and Lengthening Bar; 1 pair Dividers, 3½ inch; 1 Bow Pen, with Pencil Point; 1 Drawing Pen; 1 Protractor; 1 Key; 1 Rule. Price, each, . . . . . 2 00

**No. 90.**—Rosewood Case, with Lock and Tray, containing 14 pieces, BRASS, 1 pair Compasses, 6¼ inch, with Pen, Pencil Points, and Lengthening Bar; 1 pair Compasses, 3½ inch, with Pen and Pencil Points; 1 pair Dividers, 4¼ inch; 1 Bow Pen, with Pencil Point; 1 Drawing Pen; 2 Protractors; 1 Key; 1 Rule. Price, each, . 3 50

**No. 52.**—Rosewood Case, with Lock and Tray, containing 13 pieces, BRASS, 1 pair Compasses, 6¼ inch, with Pen, Pencil Points, and Lengthening Bar; 1 pair Dividers, 4¼ inch; 1 Bow Pen, Pencil and Needle Point; 1 Drawing Pen; 1 Protractor; 1 Proportional Divider; 1 Rule; 1 Key. Price, each, . . . . . . . . 5 00

**No. 180.**—Rosewood Case, with Lock and Tray, containing 16 pieces, GERMAN SILVER, 1 pair Compasses, 6¼ inch, with Needle Point, with Pen, Pencil Points, and Lengthening Bar; 1 pair Compasses, with Needle Point, 4¼ inch, with Pen and Pencil Point; 1 pair 4½ inch Dividers; 1 Spring Bow Pen; 1 Drawing Pen; 1 Protractor; 2 Lead Holders; 1 box Leads; 1 Rule; 1 Key. Price, . 8 00

**ALSO, A LARGE LINE OF SEPARATE INSTRUMENTS, AND OTHER ARTICLES.**

## Greene's Mineral Paste,

### For Silver-Plated Ware and Gold.

This paste does the work without scouring or scratching. Even the finest polished surfaces, which are ruined by other polishes, are left perfect where this is used.

The leading Hotels and principal Dining rooms of the country endorse this as the best, and it has found its way into thousands of homes.

Price, 4 oz. box, 25c.                    12 oz. box, 50c.

## The "Universal" Plyer.

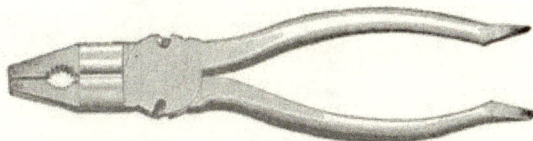

The Universal or Combination Plyer as its name implies, is a combination of several tools in one, viz: a flat nose plyer, side cutting plyer, gas plyer, nut wrench, two wire cutters, screw driver and reamer, thus making it one of the most useful tools in the market.

It is made of the finest French Steel, polished and fully warranted. Its utility is so great that it is not confined to any particular branch of trade, and is a most desirable tool for everybody.

Length, 7 inches.                    Price, $1.15.

## Edge's Bevel Back Band Saw.

All factories doing fine scroll sawing should use this style of saw—large sales and numerous testimonials justify us in offering the Bevel Back as the best Band Saw made.

| Length. | Width. | $\frac{1}{4}$ | $\frac{3}{8}$ | $\frac{1}{2}$ | $\frac{3}{4}$ |
|---|---|---|---|---|---|
| 15 ft. | | $1.50 | $1.65 | $1.90 | $2.10 |
| 16 ft. | | 1.60 | 1.75 | 2.00 | 2.25 |
| 17 ft. | | 1.70 | 1.85 | 2.15 | 2.40 |
| 18 ft. | | 1.80 | 1.95 | 2.25 | 2.50 |
| 19 ft. | | 1.90 | 2.10 | 2.40 | 2.65 |
| 20 ft. | | 2.00 | 2.20 | 2.50 | 2.80 |

# Cheap Lathe Heads.

THEY are well made and the bottoms are planed to bring the Centers in line. The No. 1 and No. 2 have Hollow Steel Head Spindles running in Cast Iron bearings. The Nos. 3 and 4 have Babbitt bearings, and the Centers are The No. 2 Morse Taper. The Cones are carefully balanced, being turned on the inside, and no better made Lathes have ever been placed upon the market. Each set of Heads consists of: 1 Head Stock, 1 Rest Socket, 1 Face Plate, 1 Common Center, 3 Bolts, 1 Tail Stock, 2 T Rests, 1 Spur Center, 2 Hand Wheel Nuts, 3 Flanges.

| No. | Swing. | No. of Speeds on Cone | Width of Belt. | Price | Price of Turned Balance Wheels including Shaft Boxes and Crank for operating Lathe by Foot Power. | | | | Price of Counter Shaft. | | |
|---|---|---|---|---|---|---|---|---|---|---|---|
| | | | | | No. | Dia. | Wgt. | Price. | No. | Size of T&L Pulleys. | Price |
| 1 | 6 in. | 2 | 1 inch. | $10.00 | 1 | 20 | 30 | $ 8.00 | 1 | 3x1 | $ 7.00 |
| 2 | 8 " | 2 | 1¼ " | 15.00 | 2 | 22 | 40 | 10.00 | 2 | 4x1½ | 8.00 |
| 3 | 11 " | 3 | 1½ " | 20.00 | 3 | 22 | 60 | 13.00 | 3 | 5x2 | 10.00 |
| 4 | 13 " | 4 | 1½ " | 30.00 | | | | | 4 | 6x3 | 12.00 |

# The "Ajax" Drill Chuck.

The Best Small Drill Chuck ever produced. Made entirely of Steel, with hardened Jaws. Holds from the smallest up to full ¼ inch Drills. Will do the work of the higher-priced Chucks. Will be sent by mail on receipt of price.

Price, $3.00 each.

# Peavey's Giant Bench Punch.

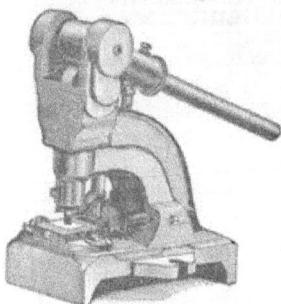

This machine is for the use of metal workers. Its power is obtained by the use of the friction roll and cam, which works either way. It is 10 inches high, 8¼ long, with lever 20 inches in length, and weighs 28 pounds.

It will punch a hole 5-16 through ¼ inch iron plate 3 inches from edge. It is neat, strong and durable.

The working parts should be kept well oiled.

#### PRICE.

| | |
|---|---|
| No. 1, with dies for one size hole, | $15.00 |
| Extra dies for round hole, per set, | .75 |

# EXTRA QUALITY AUGER BITS.

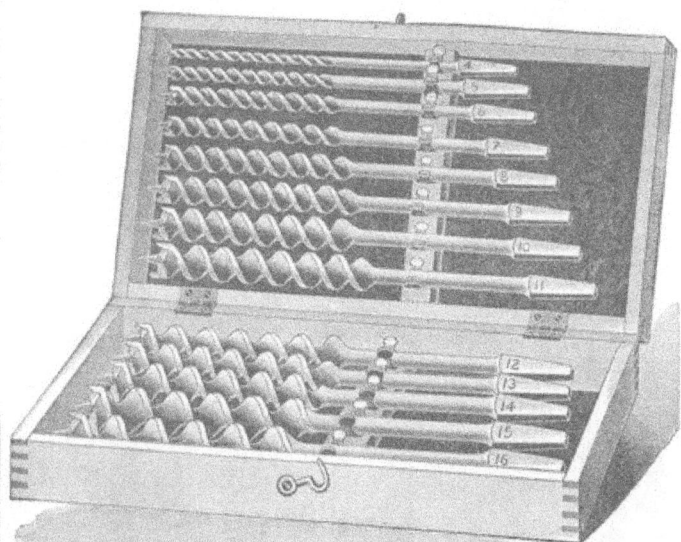

## THE FORSTNER NEW IMPROVED AUGER BIT.

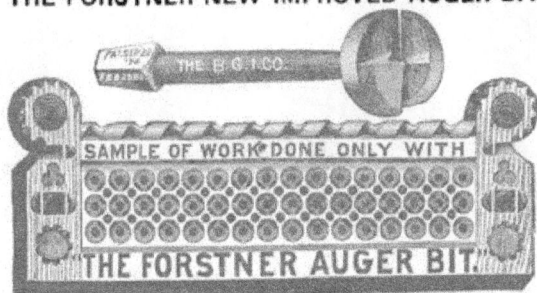

SAMPLE OF WORK DONE ONLY WITH "THE FORSTNER AUGER BIT"

Sizes:             3-8, 7-16, 4-8, 9-16, 5-8, 11-16, 6-8, 13-16, 7-8, 15-16, 8-8, 9-8 10-8, 11-8
Price Each, Brace Bit,   45c  55c 55c  68c 68c  80c 80c  92c  92c $1.05 $1.05 $1.15 $1.25 $1.35
"   "  Machine Bit, 65c  75c 75c  88c 88c $1.00 $1.00 $1.12 $1.12 $1.25 $1.25 $1.37 $1.45 $1.50

Will not deviate for knots or cracks; will bore equally well with the grain; does not split the wood, however close to the edge; makes a hole as true and polished as a Gun Barrel; is invaluable for mortising, such as letting in Door Locks, etc., as it takes the place of Chisel and Gouge, and as a Machine Bit it has no Equal.

It will bore a small hole larger, or make a hole already bored, oblong, oval or square. It will enter the wood at any angle, and from any direction, and is the only Round Bit in the world that will bore a Square Hole for letting in Bolt Heads, etc.

# TOOLS OF ALL KINDS.

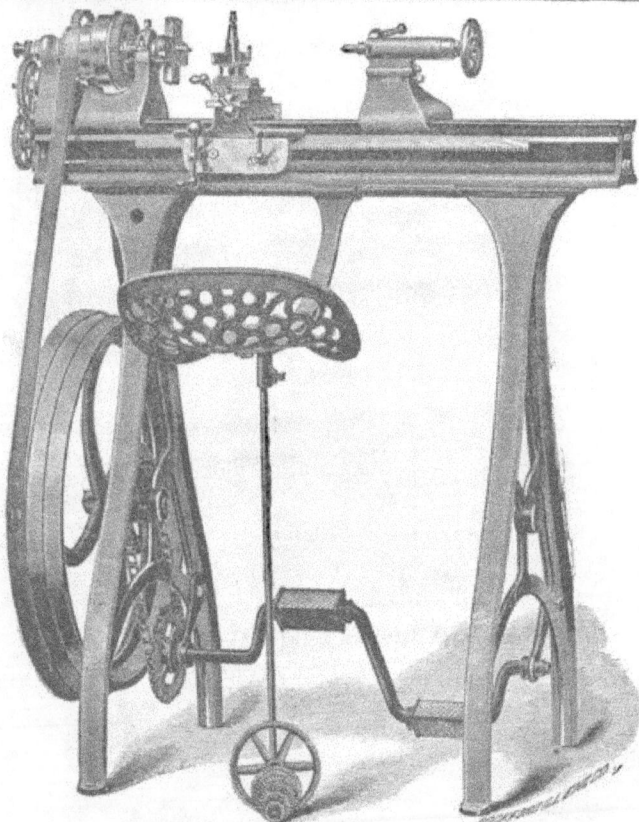

# BARNES NEW SCREW-CUTTING LATHE.

## No. 4½.

This Lathe is a back-geared, screw-cutting Lathe. It feeds right or left, and cuts screws right or left, without change of gearing. The carriage is adjustable for taper boring or ball turning. It is thoroughly gibbed for taking up wear.

The tail stock has side movement to adjust centers for turning tapers. The head stock has hollow spindle for rods up to ⅜ inch. All the gearing is cut from solid metal. All parts are made of steel where this would best serve the purpose.

It will cut all ordinary threads from 5 to 48, and miscellaneous threads up to 154. It swings 9 inches and takes 25 inches between centers. It swings 4⅝ inches over tool carriage.

The small pulley on cone is 2½ inches; the large pulley 4½. It has three speeds, and is suitably arranged for heavy or light work in turning or polishing.

The Lathe weighs 255 pounds; boxed, ready for shipment 325 pounds.

Price of the Lathe is $70.00. With old style treadle, same price.

# BENCH LATHE.

The above cut represents a small Bench Lathe which we are now manufacturing, the dimensions of which are as follows:

Bed, 24 in. long. Swing, 6½ in. Distance between Centres, 14 in. We also make the same Lathe with Bed 36 in. long, which will take between Centres 26 inches.

For light drilling and polishing, these Lathes will take the place, at a great saving in many cases, of the larger and more expensive tools in general use.

## PRICE LIST.

| | | |
|---|---|---|
| Bench Lathe, as above, with 24 in. Bed | . . . . . . . . . . | $10.00 |
| "     "     "    " 36 in. Bed | | 12.00 |
| Countershaft . . . . . . $6.00 | Extra Face Plates . . . . | .75 |
| Drill Chucks, fitted to Lathe to hold Drills from ⅛ inch, down | | 4.00 |
| Spur Centre for wood . . . . 1.00 | Screw Chuck for wood . . | 1.00 |
| Crotch Centre for drilling . . 1.00 | Drill Pad for Tail Stock . . | .75 |
| Arbor, with Nut and Flanges for Circular Saw or Emery Wheel . . . | | 1.50 |

# Improved Foot Lathe.

Fig. 1.

For Turning, Scroll and Circular Sawing, Boring, Drilling, Grooving, Polishing, etc., for the use of amateurs and artists.

This represents the Lathe with the Scroll and Circular Saw Attachments. The cut shows the Sawing Attachments thrown back, and the Lathe in position for turning.

This Lathe has been much improved since it was first put on the market, and we consider it equal to any tool made at the same price; it is now made with a Hollow Spindle, ⅜ hole, and a Drawer in the Table, without extra charge.

We have two sizes of these Lathes as follows:

No. 1 Lathe has 30 in. bed and will turn 18 in. long and 8 in. diameter. Price, with Scroll and Circular Saw Attachments, $45.

No. 2 Lathe has 48 in. bed and will turn 36 in. long and 8 in. diameter. Price, with both Scroll and Circular Saw Attachments, $55.

| | | | |
|---|---|---|---|
| Plain Lathe, with table, 30 in., | $30. | Scroll Saw Attachments, | 5. |
| "      "      "      " 48 " | 40. | Circular "      " | 10. |

## HAND RIP SAW.

This Machine will rip boards of any thickness up to 3 1-4 inches, and width to 19 inches.

The lumber is placed between two feed rollers which feed it to the saw. The feed can be made slow or fast as the operator may desire, by the cone pulleys on feed rolls. An operator can easily rip 600 feet of one-inch pine per hour.

The table is provided with an adjustable gauge to raise and lower for rabbets, bevels, etc.

Price,　　-　　-　　-　　-　　$50.00.

## LATHE No. 4.

This Lathe is designed for turning both wood and iron, and for boring, drilling, etc., etc.

It is not an amateur tool, but is strictly mechanical in every respect.

It will take in work 7 inches in diameter and 20 inches long. The leading screw for the tool carriage is operated by hand, by it the tool carriage can be travelled 20 inches. The carriage can be engaged or disengaged instantly from the screw.

The head stock spindle has taper bearings, and can be adjusted with as much delicacy as a jeweller's lathe.

Price,　　-　　-　　-　　-　　$40.00.

## LATHE No. 5.

This Lathe swings 11 inches diameter and 34 inches long, with its back gearing and cone pulleys the Lathe has a great range of speed.

It is thoroughly and substantially built, and the head stock has a 15-32 hole through its entire length.

The tool carriage is a model of convenience and accuracy, and is *gibbed* to the bed.

As a right or left screw-cutting Lathe, it is simply perfect.

Price,　　-　　-　　-　　-　　$100.00.

All the larger sizes of Lathes and Upright Drills we keep constantly in stock.

## GRINDSTONES.

(MOUNTED WITH CRANK FOR HAND.)

| Diameter, inches, | 6 | 8 | 10 | 12 |
|---|---|---|---|---|
| Price, | $1.20 | 1.50 | 1.75 | 2.00 |

## GRINDSTONES NOT MOUNTED.

| Diameter, inches, | | | 4 | 6 | 8 | 10 | 12 |
|---|---|---|---|---|---|---|---|
| Price, each, | . | . | $0.50 | .65 | .85 | 1.00 | 1.25 |

## ORANGE OIL GRINDSTONES.

| Diameter, inches, | . | . | . | . | 3 | 4 | 6 | 8 |
|---|---|---|---|---|---|---|---|---|
| Price, each, | . | . | . | . | $0.60 | .80 | 1.00 | 1.20 |

## MOUNTED GRINDSTONES.

(WITH TREADLE FOR FOOT POWER.)

| Diameter, inches, | . | . | . | . | 16 | 18 | 20 | 24 |
|---|---|---|---|---|---|---|---|---|
| Price, | . | . | . | . | $4.50 | 5.00 | 5.50 | 6.00 |

## IMPROVED IRON GRINDSTONE FRAMES.

(WITH STONE COMPLETE.)

Size of Stone, 30 × 4 inches.

Price with Pulley for Power, . $20.00

## ALSO IN STOCK:

Drills,
Taps,
Screws,
Bolts,
Vises,

Wrenches,
Cotton Waste,
Lathes,
Planers,
Chests,

Babbitt Hammers,
Copper Hammers,
Milling Cutters,
Fan Motors,
Batteries,
Rope,

Chains,
Ratchets,
Jack Screws,
Hack Saws,
Chucks,
Babbitt,
&c., &c.

Emery Grinders,
Cut Gears,
Calipers,
Dividers,
Grindstones,
Forges,
Emery Wheels,
Lathe Dogs,
Punches & Shears,
Screw Plates,
Oilers,
Circular and Band Saws,
Files.
Piano Wire,
Sheet Brass & Steel,

Brass, Copper & Steel Wire,
Brass Rod & Tubing,
Bessemer Rods,
Tool Steel,
Spring Cotters,

Iron & Copper Rivets,
Pocket Cutlery,
Skates,
Bicycles,
Tool Chests,
&c., &c.

HENRY K. BARNES

MANUFACTURER OF

OAK TANNED

Leather

Belting

LACE LEATHER

Mechanical Rubber Goods,
Fire Hose
Mill & Fire Department
Supplies
ETC.

199, 201 & 203 DEVONSHIRE ST.

104 FRANKLIN ST.

BOSTON MASS. U.S.A.